Indian Crisis

THE BACKGROUND

THE MACMILLAN COMPANY
NEW YORK · BOSTON · CHICAGO
DALLAS · ATLANTA · SAN FRANCISCO

Indian Crisis

THE BACKGROUND

by

JOHN S. HOYLAND
M.A., F.R.Hist.S.

New York
THE MACMILLAN COMPANY
1943

To
R. B. H.

CONTENTS

Indian Crisis

THE BACKGROUND

I

THE INDIAN LAND

A PHYSICAL MAP of India shows great mountains in the North, the Himalayas; lesser mountains in the East on the borders of Burma, and in the centre, the Vindhya and Satpura ranges; biggish mountains again in the South, especially the Nilgiris.

To the West, in the region of Baluchistan, there are rocky deserts; and the same cover large areas of North-western India. To the North-west, below the Himalayas, are the glorious valleys of Kashmir; the Punjab, land of the five great rivers; and farther East the immense plains through which run the Jumna, the Ganges and the Brahmaputra. In the North-east is Bengal, the "gift of its rivers."

Peninsular India is mostly highish plateau, with fertile plains round the sea-coasts. Much of it is very rocky and arid.

If we look at a political map of India, we shall see that about two-fifths of the surface is occupied by Indian States, not coloured red. They are situated across the main lines of communication in all directions. They are also along the frontiers and on or near the sea-coasts. Altogether there are 584 of them. They are not "British" India at all, but Indian India.

We notice also that there are ample communications leading up to the North-west frontier, and very few leading to the North-east. The result of this provision against possible attack from Russia, and neglect of the possibility of attack through Burma, became apparent in 1942.

We also see that, although India has a very long coast-line, there are few indentations in it, and very few good ports.

These are main reasons for the fact that with the exception of certain elements in Western India, the Indian peoples have never been seafarers.

The rivers of India have been, and are still, of supreme importance. Many of them are worshipped as sacred; and such worship bears evidence, as does the veneration of the cow in Hinduism, to elementary economic facts. Large areas are permanently dependent, and other far larger areas seasonally dependent, on the rivers for irrigation. This means that but for the rivers human life would be impossible. In the old days the rivers were also important as avenues of communication.

The ordinary Indian river shrinks to a slender flow through a vast sandy bed for eight months of the year. But for the four months of the rains the bed fills up from bank to bank, and the river will be running like an express train, perhaps half-a-mile wide.

It is a great experience to be present at one of the great religious festivals, held where two sacred rivers join. Every twelve years the most sacred place in India is believed by the Hindus to be the junction of the Jumna and the Ganges, near Allahabad. A pilgrimage to this spot at the right time may be of the highest importance to the progress of the soul, and may even relieve it from the burden of many re-births in the future. Therefore from all over India countless thousands of people, many of them aged and sick, many of them religious devotees, gather on the triangular expanse of sand where the rivers join. When I was there the English police officer in charge of traffic arrangements said that there were probably three million people gathered in that one place!

In many parts of central India the chief feature of the countryside is the jungle. It is both beautiful and terrible. There are fierce beasts in it. The men that live in the jungle are very shy, and very poor. They are apt to fall victim to disastrous epidemics, as in the pneumonia of 1918, or the cholera of 1921.

Famine is an enemy never far out of sight. The tiny villages in which they live lie long distances apart, and their fields are decimated by wild creatures, especially pig, deer and flocks of parrots. But they are an intensely lovable people; and their tribal customs and beliefs are often of very great interest.

Through these jungle-regions run fairly high mountain ranges. In some districts there are extremely deep ravines, with precipitous sides, and deep water at the bottom, in which one may swim. The discovery of new routes down into these ravines, and the exploring of the caves which the water has worn deep underground, give opportunities for adventurous holidays to those who like that sort of thing.

There are also sacred mountains in many parts of India. Some of these have great temples on the top. But in the remoter districts there will be no permanent inhabitants, except perhaps a hermit or two, living a solitary life of great austerity amongst the wild beasts. There is often a yearly pilgrimage to such sacred mountains, up which the weak and aged are carried, under conditions of great difficulty and danger, in the hope of attaining merit for the loosening of the necessity for re-birth.

On other high mountains in central India there are magnificent ruins of hill-fortresses. Some of these, like Asirgarh, are really deserted cities, with very strong fortifications round them. The massive nature of their fortifications gives the visitor an insight into political conditions in the age in which they were built; and the ruined palaces which stand inside the walls give one some idea also of the social conditions of that age.

Houses in India vary from the most modern type of structure in the big cities to the flimsiest of palm-leaf, mud-and-wattle, or bamboo huts in the villages. During the past two centuries the poor have been rapidly becoming poorer in India, and not only on account of the tremendous rise of population. The housing of the poorest of the poor nowadays is almost incredibly primitive. In the great cities there are big slum areas, where the congestion is frightful, and the people live in tightly-crammed tenements or in tiny hovels, with appalling sanitary conditions all around.

On the other hand there are magnificent palaces belonging to the well-to-do, especially to Princes, great landholders and successful money-lenders. And in many of the cities there are great modern factories, so that India has become the eighth most important country in the world from the point of view of industry.

In spite of the teeming population, the countryside of India, as soon as one is clear of the great cities, seems only sparsely populated. Bitter experiences in the past have taught the people the advantages of living closely together in villages, where they may combine to resist attack, instead of living in scattered farm-houses, as in the West. Consequently the Indian land-scape generally appears almost empty except for distant villages each embowered in its grove of trees. Here and there one may see a farmer at work in his fields, perhaps with his wife and his children sharing in his labour. When the crops are ripening, the people leave their villages for a time, and live amongst the fields in little temporary sheds, sometimes elevated on four poles so as to give watchers a clear view over the crops. From these points of vantage a keen look-out is kept day and night for parrots, pig, deer and other marauders. The life of the Indian agriculturalist is hard, especially at such seasons, but it is a fine open-air life.

The villages and small towns are the true India, because it is in them that the vast majority of the population is to be found. The present writer lived for a considerable period in a small country town. Each street is flanked by the houses and shops of the families who practise one particular trade, and therefore belong (for the most part) to one "caste." I lived in the street inhabited by the makers of brass vessels; and from long before dawn till long after dark the musical clink of their hammers was to be heard. A great deal of very lovely and artistic work was performed in that street, under very primitive conditions. Another street was occupied by goldsmiths and silversmiths; another by blacksmiths; another by carpenters; another by grain-dealers; and so on. Close outside the town was a famous old ruined fort, in the middle of which a well-equipped modern High School had been built. In another direction close outside the town was a Government hospital. A little farther out were the law-courts. Close around the town, but away from the noise and smells, were the houses of the more well-to-do citizens, chiefly lawyers, with a few schoolmasters and doctors. The Moslems lived chiefly in a special area of the town, and the outcastes, who performed the essential function of scavengers, in another area. The whole community was very much like what a mediaeval town must have been in the West, the place of the central Church or Cathedral being taken by a group of finely-built temples ranged along the top of a broad flight of stone steps leading down into the waters of one of the sacred rivers.

Well outside the town and, except for telegraph wires, almost the only sign of modern life, lay the railway station.

In the centre of the town, on a broad open space, the market was held. To this market villagers from long distances round brought their produce; and on the right day one could purchase all manner of interesting and beautiful examples of Indian handicraft.

It was dangerous to venture far into the forests which covered the hills to the north of the town, because of the chance of meeting a tiger; and it was even dangerous to walk along the river-side in the cool of the evening. An old friend of mine set out for such a walk one evening, and never returned. From the very scanty remains that were found, it was clear that a crocodile hiding in a gully of the sandy bed of the river had attacked and killed him.

Every now and then the life of a community such as that in this small town is shaken by plague or famine. If it is plague, the whole town has to be evacuated at the briefest notice and the inhabitants take up their residence in roughly-built shelters erected in the fields all around. This is because the plague is carried by the rats which swarm in the town itself. The sudden dying of these rats in inconvenient places acts as a danger-signal of the coming of the disease, which is so dreadful in its effect that the people have learnt to carry out the evacuation policy thoroughly and speedily.

In time of famine things are much better nowadays than they were: for Government sets to work to bring in food supplies and to open relief works where the unemployed (and every Indian agriculturalist is unemployed for some four months in the year, owing to climatic conditions) may earn the wherewithal to purchase provisions.

In a very serious epidemic, such as a cholera-wave or the pneumonia of 1918, the life of such a country-town community is shaken to its foundations. Many of the inhabitants fly to unknown destinations, taking the disease with them; and amongst those who remain panic shatters the framework of caste-society.

II

NATURE IN INDIA

IN OUR SOFT Western climate we are wont to think of Nature as a beneficent force, providing us with succulent vegetables, with spring flowers in pleasing variety, with song-birds, and with picturesque sunsets.

Things are different in India. There Nature is fierce, dangerous, and tyrannical. She sends a great variety of wild beasts, which in an average year kill something like thirty thousand people. She sends earthquakes, which in a few seconds flatten towns (and the people living in them) over a whole wide province, destroy agriculture by covering the fields with sand from underground, and alter the levels of the land, so that next rainy season the rivers overflow and drown thousands of people.

Nature sends drought, which may continue year after year till first the cattle die, and then the men. Nature sends appalling pestilences, frightful hail-storms which beat the growing crops into the earth, floods which destroy a thousand villages in a night. Nature is not gracious and beneficent, but deadly. She may have kindly elements in her character; but the traits which force themselves most prominently upon the attention of simple people are traits which show her as a vast reservoir of destruction. She is to be placated, if possible, so that she may hold her hand, and not wipe out humankind in a capricious mood of wanton destructiveness.

These dangerous aspects of Nature are at the root of a great deal of Indian religion, especially amongst the animistic tribes in the forest areas, and the worshippers of Shiva. The early

7

literature of India, beginning with the Vedas, great poems written three thousand years ago, show many traces of the altered attitude towards Nature which appeared as the Aryan invaders realized how different she was in India to what she had been in the more temperate lands from which they came.

The ordinary European, arriving for the first time in India, is inevitably impressed by one thing, the heat. He finds himself, if he is lucky enough to be stationed somewhere where electricity is available, quite ridiculously dependent upon an electric fan. During a large part of the year, if he is to do any decent amount of work by day, or get any decent amount of sleep by night, he must keep within the radius of the fan's ministrations. Otherwise the sweat pours from him; he becomes unbearably irritable; and at night he tosses sleepless from side to side, in an inferno, a bed of fire, where the touch of the sheets or the pillow scorches his flesh. It is true that in the northern parts of India there is a brief "cold-weather," during which it is not uncommon for water actually to freeze, and the heat-grilled Englishman feels the cold with penetrating misery, whilst the poorer Indians shiver all night, unable to sleep for cold, over miserable little fires of sticks or cow-dung. But this cold weather is very soon over; and the heat returns, seemingly more dreadful than ever before because of the brief respite that has been enjoyed.

For all her terrors, Indian Nature is very beautiful, especially at night, when the stars shine with a radiance quite unbelievable to anyone who has not lain awake out in the open, gazing up at the night-sky. The moonlight also is of a strange shimmering vividness unknown in the West. And as for the Indian dawn. . . .

Then there are the mountains, and the forests, with the rich glory of golden sunshine over everything.

It is hard, however, in these forests to forget the presence of wild beasts. Whenever there is a prolonged drought, the deer on which the tigers normally feed, migrate *en masse* for very long distances to parts of the country where green things are still to be found for eating. For some reason the tigers do not move also, but turn to human flesh. I have lived, during famine time, in a district completely terrorized by man-eaters. So many people had been killed that finally the peasants would not leave their villages till 10 o'clock in the morning, and were back again soon after two in the afternoon. The mid-day hours, when the tigers are generally asleep, were the only time when the people might with comparative safety go out to try to till their fields, to pasture their cattle, or to travel from remote villages to market-towns. Since the villages in that area were mostly some 15 miles apart, buried in almost pathless and very hilly jungle, this meant that communications practically broke down, and that the agricultural life of the district almost came to a standstill. The surviving cattle suffered very severely also, since there was no time, during those mid-day hours, to take them far enough afield to get sufficient pasture. Worst of all was the panic bred in the poor jungle-dwellers by the activity of so many man-eaters all around them. Fear can kill, as one realizes at such a time.

Monkeys are an appalling pest in some parts of India, especially in the northern cities, such as Muttra and Delhi. They are sacred animals, and so they may not be shot. In these large cities they commit widespread depredations, stealing all manner of things from shops and houses. In the country districts they also sometimes do very serious damage to crops. A friend of mine in Delhi suffered acutely from the monkeys. They used to come right into his house, seize anything they could find, and retire to the roof, where they either ate the stolen object, if it was in any way eatable, or tore it to pieces if it was not. On one occasion a large and formidable monkey entered my friend's bathroom, and removed from it a bottle of pills, which he proceeded to eat one by one on the roof, tipping them out of the bottle in a very human way. In this manner the large monkey went right through the bottle of pills. My friend's only consolation lay in the fact that they were Cascara pills! He finally got rid of those monkeys by arranging a large number of particularly explosive Roman candles under the tree in which they roosted at night, and letting them all off at the same moment. The monkeys left tumultuously in the midst of a galaxy of exploding stars, and never returned!

One large city was so tormented by monkeys that men were appointed to go round and catch them in enormous butterfly-net contraptions. They were then decanted into covered rail-way-vans, and shipped to a small station in the depths of the jungle far away. Unfortunately reverence for life did not extend to the provision of food and water for the journey, with disastrous results to at least half of the travellers.

The "smaller horrors of war" are also found in great profusion in India, in almost as great profusion indeed as in some slum districts of our own country. You find them on railway journeys; and you find them in houses. I remember taking some tourists just out from England to visit a very holy and very distinguished old gentleman, and watching the live-stock gradually emerge from the cracks in the chairs on which the visitors were seated, and ascend to a more intimate acquaint-ance with their persons! And there are other memories. . . .

Snakes add another type of zest to life. I was once attending a very solemn meeting when a small but exceedingly poisonous snake made its appearance in the open doorway. It was of a variety whose bite is supposed to prove fatal, under unpleasant circumstances, in twenty minutes. No one else saw the in-truder, and being the youngest member of the party I did not like to make a disturbance; but as soon as the others noticed it, the meeting broke up in disorder, shoes were snatched off, and were used as clubs to despatch the snake!

I also remember being called from a dinner-party by an agitated friend, whose house had just been entered by a cobra. The snake had taken up its abode behind a chest in the corner of a room, and could only be dealt with by lying flat on the floor, arranging a semi-circle of lamps, and then taking a pot-shot. The cobra came out practically in two pieces, but still game, and a very awkward situation (for me) was saved by another member of the party, who had had the sense to arm himself with a big stick, and to take up his station to one side of the chest.

Mad dogs are exceedingly common in India, and worse still, mad jackals. One took refuge in my pantry in 1922, and had to be dealt with there, a most unpleasant experience. Nowadays it is possible to get anti-rabic treatment in all the big centres of population; but thirty years ago it was needful to travel at once, if one were bitten, to a certain hill-station in the Hima-layas. I remember on one occasion seeing a long, open railway carriage packed with people who had all been bitten by one mad jackal, and had received free passes to the hill-station in question for anti-rabic treatment.

But it is in times of pestilence that one feels most acutely the savage power of Indian Nature. In 1918 the contrast was very noticeable between the indescribable glories of the noontide forest and the horrors of the forest villages, where from every hut could be heard the sharp, rasping breathing of people in the last stages of pneumonia. In one such village was a man who had lost, one after another, his wife and all his nine children. He had himself been desperately ill; and all he could do with their bodies was to drag them to the edge of a dry watercourse, and push them over the edge. Some of the villages were entirely desolate. At others the people had left their houses and were lying out in the open, in the fields, ill with the universal pneu-monia. We lost 8 per cent. of the population in three weeks in the district where I was working at that time.

Or there was the cholera epidemic which followed famine

conditions in the North-eastern area of the Central Provinces in 1921. Very few people died that year of actual starvation, owing to the admirable manner in which the Famine Code, perfected during the appalling famines at the beginning of the century, was found to work. But thousands upon thousands died of the cholera which followed the famine. I well remember the news arriving of the outbreak at a distant village of what from the description sounded like cholera. The report turned out to be true, and in less than a week it had spread everywhere over the famine district. One symptom of cholera is a raging thirst. The victims of the disease would crawl, or get themselves carried, to the nearest well or waterhole, and would pollute the water even before their death. There was no other source of water in the raging heat of May. No wonder that the cholera spread! Along the tracks through the jungle one would find cholera victims lying dead. They had crawled there from villages deep in the jungle, in the hope that some passer-by might give them help. After a night out in the open air, one would awake to find a bullock-cart near by, with its driver dead of cholera in it. He had died in the course of a night-journey, and his bullocks had carried him forward till they came near human beings.

Under such conditions a jungle population rapidly sinks into hopelessness and apathy. It is very hard to get them to do anything to save themselves, even to take the most elementary precautions, such as boiling drinking-water. This is especially so if they are at the same time terrorized by the presence of formidable man-eating tigers in the forests around their villages. At such times one comes to understand the mentality of people who regard Nature-forces as terrors to be placated rather than as beneficent powers with which man may cooperate.

III

SALIENT FACTORS IN THE
HISTORY OF INDIA

A FAMOUS AMERICAN not long ago declared that "History is Bunk"; his attitude would be impossible in India, where history is a living force visibly existing all around one. In any collection of school children in the Central Provinces, for instance, the most casual observer will at once notice certain clearly-marked types of humanity; there are aboriginals, with broad noses, thick lips and very dark complexions; many of them look almost like negroes, except that they do not have curly hair. They are descendants of the original pre-Aryan population of the whole of India, though their tribes are now only to be found in remote and jungle districts. There will probably be a few Dravidians from the South, also with very dark skins, but thin aristocratic faces. They represent a population which may have come originally, a very long time ago, from Mesopotamia, either through the passes of the Northwest, or by sea to the South-western coast. There will also be a few representatives of a Mongolian type, from Bengal or beyond, with high cheek-bones, eyes of a somewhat Chinese appearance, and a complexion which is often rather yellow than brown. Their forefathers entered India, very long ago, through the passes of the North-east. There are now scores of millions of their descendants in the Eastern parts of India. Again there will be a sprinkling of representatives of the Arab or Semitic type, with hooked noses, thin faces, and fairly light complexion. They will be descendants of the Islamic conquerors who began to enter India in the eighth century, and for many centuries held imperial control over almost the whole country. Then there will be Brahmins, descendants of the Aryan invaders of some three thousand five hundred years ago, who came from Central Asia, bringing with them a language akin to Latin and Greek, the ancient Sanskrit, and the joyous nature-worship which is shown in the early Vedic writings. Their distant descendants to-day are often of an almost European type of physique, including the complexion, because of the racial purity ensured by the caste-system. Much more numerous will be the representatives of the various degrees of intermixture between the Aryan invaders and the aboriginal, Mongolian and Dravidian peoples whom they conquered. There is one especially notable type, that of the Marathas, short, stalwart, fairly dark in complexion, the last great ruling race (with the exception of the Sikhs in the North-west) before the British gained control of India.

Such an assembly is living history; and the heritage received by each of these various groups presents its own problems for the contemporary well-being of India.

The aboriginal tribes, the only real "natives" of India, were ruled in the past by tribal chieftains; but their "medicine men" or "witch doctors" had very great power (and in outlying regions have it still). These tribes are now deplorably poor and ignorant, living in inaccessible areas, under the sway of a great variety of forms of spirit-worship. In some districts they took, ages ago, to criminal practices, which have become traditional with them. In consequence they still give great trouble to constituted authorities. Methods of practical friendship have of recent years proved the best means of taming them. They have been induced to settle and to practise handicrafts; but wise and tactful leadership, in a spirit of brotherhood, has proved essential if they are to be kept on the right track.

In many of the more prosperous parts of the country the

Untouchables are descendants of the primitive aboriginal population. They have been submerged by successive waves of invaders, and have been reduced to the necessity of performing the lowest menial services for their conquerors, especially that of scavenging. They are regarded by many orthodox Hindus as sub-human, and are treated accordingly, being forbidden to use public wells, buildings or streets, if there is any chance of contact with members of the higher sections of society (i.e., with caste Hindus). Mr. Gandhi has felt that their present position is not merely a disgrace to India, but is a dangerous threat to her freedom and unity for the future. Consequently he has made the removal of Untouchability—that is, the belated doing of justice to the conquered aboriginal population—one of the main planks in his platform of social and political reform.

As the Aryan invaders descended from the mountains of the North-west, occupied the Ganges valley, pressed through the central belt of forest and mountain, and finally conquered even the extreme South, they settled everywhere into States ruled either by a semi-elective kingship, or by groups of elders forming a kind of aristocratic republicanism.* In these States a brilliant culture developed, focused in the magnificent religious and philosophical literature of the Vedic and post-Vedic periods. Women enjoyed a position of dignity and power. The gods of the Aryans were personifications of the great powers of Nature, the sky, the rain, the fire, the storm, the dawn, the rays of sunrise, the sun himself, the wind, the day. In the worship of Varuna, god of the sky, the Aryans came very near to monotheism, or rather perhaps to what Max Müller called by the queer name of "henotheism," the worship of one god alone

---

* The great epics, the *Mahabharata* and the *Ramayana*, show the Aryans at different stages of this advance. It must be noticed that at least a thousand years before the coming of the Aryans, a brilliant and highly artistic culture, in close touch with that of Sumeria, existed in the Indus valley in the North-West.

supreme over all others, though the existence of these others is not denied. Varuna is the Greek Ouranos, the sky, and thus his name reminds us how close are the origins of European and Indian words as well as worships. Of him a Vedic hymn says, "Thou art lord of all, of heaven and earth; thou art king of all those who are gods, and of all those who are men."

It was in these Aryan kingdoms and republics that the caste system first developed. Its Sanskrit name means "colour-bar," and it probably originated as a practical method of keeping the Aryan blood pure from intermixture with the black aborigines. In time the Aryans themselves became divided into three main castes, the Brahmins or priests, the Kshattriyas or warriors, the Vaisyas or merchants and farmers. Beneath these three castes, which were regarded as "twice-born," there was a fourth caste, the Sudras, for the aboriginals and other serfs.* They were held to be "once-born." As time went on these main caste divisions became infinitely subdivided. In the main each caste kept to a separate function performed (ideally at least) on behalf of the community and in the service of God. Hence there is a blacksmith caste, a washerman caste, a weaver caste. Rigid barriers grew up between caste and caste. There must be no intermarriage. There must be no taking of food or water from the hands of a man of lower caste. In some parts of India even the falling of the shadow of a low-caste man across a high-caste man is held to defile.

In the sixth century before Christ, in one of these Aryan states, the greatest of all Indians was born, Gautama the Buddha (the enlightened one). He was the son of a chieftain, brought up in luxury; but his threefold vision of the meaning of the world's pain sent him out, a religious mendicant and ascetic, to search for the secret of the conquest of suffering. Long before this, the early brightness and hopefulness of the Vedic

* In South India the Dravidians mainly become Sudras, and the aboriginals were relegated to an "outcaste" or "fifth" (*panchama*) position lower still.

religion had become clouded, partly through contact with aboriginal cults, partly perhaps as a result of existence beneath the despotic and terrifying sway of Nature as she is in India. Men had begun to think of life as a burden, not a blessing; and at the same time the belief had gained ground that the soul is destined to return again and again to this world, in birth after birth, carrying forward each time the totality of evil and of good that is the result of action. It was (and still is) believed that by an immutable law of the universe evil must be punished and good rewarded. The soul has to return to bear the punishment or enjoy the reward. Already great philosophical and religious systems had begun to develop, teaching that by right ritual observance (especially sacrifice to the gods), or by right absorption in the knowledge of the Absolute Reality, the soul may be set free from the necessity of re-birth and therefore from suffering. This latter method is called the way of Release by Knowledge (Gnyan). Gautama Buddha taught another way of Release, that of rightness of spirit and conduct. It was a way open to all men, of whatever caste (previous philosophies of Release had tended to be class-conscious and exclusive); and it did not demand the propitiation of vast numbers of deities by sacrifice and ritual. In fact Buddha taught nothing definite about the gods, with the result that a few generations after his death men who had embraced his Way of Release through mercy, good-will, rightness of spirit and conduct, began to be driven by an irresistible impulse to worship as a god Gautama himself.

The Buddhist age lasted in all for about fifteen hundred years, from the sixth century before Christ to the tenth century A.D., though during the latter part of that long period Hinduism was busy re-absorbing Buddhism. A magnificent Buddhist literature sprang up, and an even more magnificent Buddhist art, the latter centred at first in the wonderful rock-cut shrines and palaces which are still to be seen in many parts of India.

Early in that period came the lightning-raid of Alexander the Great and his conquest of the Panjab and of Sind, which brought a permanent Greek influence into North-western Buddhist sculpture and art. Later there came the great All-India Buddhist Empire, ruled by pacifist methods under the famous pacifist Emperor Asoka. Afterwards India was split up into various kingdoms, some strong, some weak. There was much warfare. There were invasions by wild tribes from Central Asia. Later, pressure began to be felt from Islamic invaders in the West. Thus Indian civilization suffered shock after shock. Buddhism began to decay, and became deeply affected by the worship of gods and demons.

Meanwhile Hinduism had developed another way of Release, perhaps the most significant of all. It was the way of personal devotion to a personal god. In the glorious Song of the Lord (the Bhagavadgita, which is often called for simplicity's sake the *Gita* or "Song"), Krishna was set forth as the object of devoted worship and obedience. The true worshipper is to do his duty, within the caste-system, as a member of the community, and is to do everything in the spirit of devotion to the Saviour-God, Krishna.* It was a message which spoke direct to the common man, demanding neither elaborate and expensive ritual observances, nor a retirement from the world and the cultivation of philosophical abstraction, nor austere correctness of spirit and conduct. It was a warm and personal religion, not even resolutely pacifist, as Buddhism had been and later phases of Hinduism were to become. From that time forward † the school of religion called *Bhakti* (personal devotion) became more and more popular and more and more influential in Indian history.

Towards the end of the Buddhist period there was a notable revival and restatement of the Way of Knowledge, chiefly under the leadership of the great teacher Shankara. Release

* The corresponding Saviour-God in the *Ramayana* is Rama.
† The *Gita* was probably written in the century before Christ.

from re-birth is only to be found as the soul gathers itself closely together, gazes inward, and realizes—in a place beyond all action, good or bad—that it is one with the Absolute Reality.

Hinduism was thus doubly revived; and the corrupt and feeble remnants of Buddhism were steadily assimilated into the wide inclusiveness of the Hindu religious and philosophical system. Great Hindu art, especially in architecture and sculpture, had begun to appear long before the final disappearance of Buddhism in the tenth century after Christ. Much of this art was profoundly symbolical, different aspects of Hindu teaching being typified by almost every detail in the attitude for instance of a sculptured figure.

It was upon an India divided into a large number of Hindu kingdoms, frequently hostile to each other, that the frightful tornado of the main Moslem attack broke, late in the tenth century. At first it was a question of terribly destructive raids, but soon these raids were seen to be the prelude to Moslem imperialism. First the North-west, then the North, then the East, and much later the South also, became areas first barbarously conquered, and then despotically ruled, by a long succession of invaders from Central Asia, all bound together and immensely invigorated by their common allegiance to the unflinching monotheism and the detestation of all idolatry, taught by Mohammed. During these centuries of oppression the true history of India is a history of the spirit, marked by the rise of teacher after teacher to greatness and eminence (Ramanuja and Ramananda are the best known), and the appearance all over the country, but especially in Bengal and in Western India, of ever fresh revivals of *Bhakti* religion.

From early in the sixteenth century to early in the eighteenth most of India was loosely united under the feudal sway of the Moghal Empire. The great Emperor Akbar, although nominally a devout Moslem, bound his millions of Hindu subjects to him in affectionate regard, because of his tolerance and large-heartedness. These qualities made his reign genuinely glorious. He was followed, however, after an interval, by the fanatical bigot Aurangzeb, whose persecution utterly estranged the Hindus. Then came the successful revolt of the Marathas. In the meanwhile Aurangzeb had been wasting his strength in attacks on Moslem kingdoms in peninsular India—kingdoms which had once been feudatory to the Moghal Empire, but had asserted their independence. The result was the break-up of the Moghal Empire.

For generations before this, the Europeans had been arriving in India, first the Portuguese, then the Dutch, the French, the British. They came to trade, and remained to conquer. During the eighteenth century a prolonged struggle took place between the French, long under the leadership of the brilliant Dupleix, and the British power organized by the East India Company. The commercial, and other, morality of the Company's servants will frequently not bear examination by modern standards; but they could fight. The French were beaten, then the Marathas, then the Sikhs (by the middle of the nineteenth century), each by the help of a different company of Indian princes as allies. By way of reward such princes received from the Company treaties granting them security, and British support, in the retaining of their States. Hence was born one of the major problems of modern India.

Finally, towards the end of the nineteenth century, and a generation after the Mutiny had brought Company rule to an end, came the founding, with the effective help and support of certain distinguished Westerners, of the Indian National Congress. In the first quarter of the twentieth century the Congress became the focus of Indian aspirations, first for Dominion Status within the British Commonwealth of Nations, and then for independent nationhood. The true gift of British imperialism to India was seen in the new sense of national unity and in the new demand for national liberty.

IV

INDIAN PERSONALITY

IF WE IN the West are ever to understand India, it is highly necessary that we should be able to look upon individual members of the Indian population as friends; and Indians have a great and splendid capacity both for friendship and for responding to friendship.

One of the first Indians whom I got to know in the way of friendship was the distinguished old gentleman, Pandit Balwant Singh, who took me through long and delightful vistas of the *Ramayana* of Tulsi Das. Slowly and patiently he introduced me to the Indian point of view as shown in that wonderfully tender, and at the same time adventurous, epic poem. All the while I was gaining something even more valuable from him than these lessons, a knowledge coming from contact with himself of the peculiarly gracious and beautiful type of personality which is bred in a man who has spent a long life not only in the study of the deep things of the spirit, as they are set forth in Hindu philosophy, but also in simple *Bhakti*-devotion to a Saviour-god, Rama, the hero of the *Ramayana*.

Then there was the North Indian student, an Indian Christian, who came South to help me with the study of Hindustani. From him I learnt what it is like to be a member of a subject race, but at the same time to be inspired by a universal ideal. His Christianity had gained from its Indian environment a warmth of tone, and a spiritual depth which are rare in the West; but at the same time he felt the wrongs and degradations of his country with a burning sense of shame, which occasionally made relationships difficult between the representative (by complexion at any rate) of the conquering race, and the representative of the conquered. It is essential sooner or later to learn what these big-scale political facts mean from the experience of friendship with such a man, who by his position is heir both to the Christian world-culture and to the sufferings of a proud and sensitive people groaning under foreign imperialism.

Then there was my lawyer friend. He had lived long in England in his younger days, and was a distinguished Liberal (or "Moderate") in the Provincial Legislative Assembly. He kept up to date with modern movements of thought. But as his years increased, he turned more and more to his study and practice of the Hindu way of life. After his busy day's work in the Law-courts, I would see him sitting during the evening hours, on the little concrete base of a railway signal, by the side of the line. Close to his hand would be a copy of one of the ancient Hindu Scriptures, but it would have been laid aside after a brief reading, and he would have turned to the practice of *samadhi*, contemplation. He would sit there, perhaps for hours, with his legs crossed, and his eyes closed; his European dress would have been laid aside with the day's work, and he would be in Indian garb; to one side of him the trains were rattling past, and to the other side was a busy street; but he was totally undisturbed by such extraneous things, as he practised in this way the presence of the Unseen Reality.

Then there was the Indian Christian doctor, who had worked very hard, and at great expense, in acquiring professional qualifications which set him at the head of a vocation whose services are more bitterly needed than those of any other profession in modern India. When he was at last fully equipped, he turned his back on all the brilliant prospects of dignity, advancement and wealth, which were opening out before him, and went to live and work amongst the poorest of the poor, that he might do something to raise his outcaste fellow-countrymen from their misery and filth. He was a man whose friendship had in it a peculiar aroma of Christlikeness; and from him and others like him I have learnt to be doubtful whether we shall ever know what Christlikeness, or Christ Himself, mean till India has come to understand Him and reinterpret Him to the materialistic West.

Then there was my colleague, a devout and deeply-read Hindu, with a wide knowledge of the Indian historical heritage, and boundless ambitions for the Indian future. One day he lost his only son, and I tried to comfort him. He was grateful for my clumsily-expressed sympathy; but at the end he said, "Yes, he and I loved each other very much; but we are like travellers who, coming from different directions, have met and talked together for a time on a great highroad. Now we have parted, and gone each his own way; and we shall never, never meet again!" He gave me perhaps my first real insight into the heart-hunger of India, the heart-hunger caused by her universal belief in re-incarnation. She has evolved her great systems of Release, by due performance of ritual and sacrifice, by knowledge of Oneness with the Absolute Reality, by rightness of spirit and conduct, by personal devotion to a Saviour-god. But deep beneath these there is still the grief which refuses to be comforted so long as the belief in re-incarnation remains. The soul that returns bears no attributes with it by which it may be known and loved once more; it merely brings the weight of *karma*, action performed in past incarnations, for which reward and punishment must be endured. It can never meet again those who have loved it. Once more, it is impossible to realize what these things mean till you find and know them in the experience of a human being who is your friend.

Then there were a long succession of student friends, from whom I learned far more than I could teach. There was the boy with whom I read through the whole of Shakespeare, one unendurably sultry hot-weather. I gained from him, day after scorching day, as we sat in the coolest place we could find, some knowledge of how the characteristics of Western humanity, drawn by the greatest artist of all time, look to a fully-awakened intelligence nurtured in the Indian heritage. I learned how much drops away as tawdry and superficial, even from Shakespeare's greatest characters; how keenly hidden motives may be detected and their influence traced; how penetrating and sensitive is the psychological insight of the trained Hindu mind.

Then there was that other student-friend, during those electric days of Gandhi's arrest, early in 1922. A few years before, on the mere rumour of Government's interfering with the great man's freedom (a rumour which turned out to be ill-founded), there had been widespread rioting, and in the Northwest a movement had started which was widely interpreted as the outbreak of insurrection, and had been accompanied by great loss of life. But now, when the arrest had actually taken place, there had hardly been a murmur of expostulation from any part of India. Gandhi's position in the hearts of his people was immeasurably stronger than it had been in 1919; and yet there had been this utter impassivity all over India in face of his arrest. What could it mean? Everywhere, even in the most isolated positions, the lives of English people had been completely secure. There had been no rioting, no signs of resentment. I asked my friend, in bewilderment, what was the reason for this extraordinary quiet. He replied, "It was by his orders; he told us to make no move against the English, whatever happened to himself; and we have obeyed." I caught from that student a conception of the immense significance of national discipline, imposed on so vast and so unlettered a population, by their love and devotion to the leader whom already they were beginning to regard as an embodiment of the Supreme Good-will.

Then there was another student, a great cricketer, who had

been thrown off his mental balance by the excitement of the political events at the time of the starting of the Non-Cooperation movement. He had taken a false step, which might have led himself and others into grave trouble; but it had been possible to set things right, and to keep the matter a secret. A little later it had been possible also to save him from tuberculosis. The result was a deep and enduring affection, from which there was much to be learnt of what friendship may mean, and effect, in relation to Indian problems.

There were the nine Indian Christian schoolboys, with whom we planned and carried through the distribution of medicines and medical advice in a remote and jungly district, during the pneumonia epidemic of 1918. One or two of them were as young as fourteen. They had all recently been ill themselves with the influenza which was the prelude to the pneumonia. They had ample opportunities of observing what the disease meant. But they—the only volunteers that could be found for the dangerous and arduous job—went through with it, faithfully and courageously, covering many hundreds of miles, between them, of very difficult country, and undoubtedly saving many lives. The group of us became a living unity, a single weapon for the conquest of an appalling evil. No one who has not lived through such an experience can realize what it means to be a work in a group like this, a group in which differences of race, culture, antecedents, vanish as a new corporate personality emerges in and through action of good-will against evil.

Then there were friends of another sort. The old man, member of an aboriginal tribe, who used to take my letters to the post-office, and bring back monies from the bank. He could only count on his fingers; this gave him ten, plus ten on his toes; that made twenty, which was the limit of his arithmetic, except that by repeating the process he could get as far as twenty twenties. He therefore could, and did, bring any sum up to four hundred rupees safe home. If it were a question of more than that, two journeys were required! He was absolutely faithful and honest, and could be trusted implicitly with any valuables. He was also extremely witty; and he always cracked a joke with me before he set off on his errands. From him I got to know something of the mind and the lovableness of the aboriginal tribesmen; and that is knowledge worth knowing, and hard enough to come by in the ordinary course.

Then there was Daulat, the *chaprassi*, or porter and messenger, at the institution which I served. Since I returned to England he has kept up more of a correspondence with me than anyone else. He was, and is, extraordinarily intelligent, though he knows hardly any English. Quietly and tactfully he directed my footsteps amongst many difficulties. He was always ready and willing to undertake fresh bits of work. He never complained. He was an invaluable smoother-over of awkward situations.

Then there are the Great Ones:—Rabindranath Tagore, with his unforgettable dignity of carriage and appearance, his deep tuneful voice, as he read his poems to us; Mahatma Munshi Ram, later a martyr to his religious faith, but once leader of the extraordinarily interesting group of men who made the Arya Samaj training-college near Hardwar a force to be reckoned with in modern India; the right Hon. G. K. Gokhale, a man dying by inches, but the finest orator I have ever listened to in the English language, and in private a leader who inspired everyone who came in contact with him with his own passionate belief in the great future of his country; Sadhu Sundar Singh, the Christlike apostle of Tibet; above all, Mahatma Gandhi, first as I struggled to protect him from the eagerness of an immense mob of his followers, who seemed about to surge over him and trample him into the dust (he himself was totally unperturbed); then later as he was when he walked by my side—three enormous detectives close behind—

and told me in the dawn how poverty and unemployment may be conquered, and spoke prophetically of the value and meaning of community-life.

There is a type of mind which approaches things Indian from the point of view of the superior white man. This type of mind will learn nothing from India, and in view of things Japanese is even more fatuous to-day than it has ever been before.

There is another type of mind which is gushingly sentimental in its reactions to India and Indians. They are all wonderful, and the Oriental view-point is always right. Modern India does not want sentiment, but fair dealing and practical friendship.

We have to recognize, if we ourselves are from the West, that the average Indian is psychologically much more sensitive and much more subtle than ourselves; that he is far more closely aware of spiritual values and of issues that appear meaningless to a wholy materialistic world-view; that he has a great capacity for friendship; that he may be led, but if so it must be from alongside; that he can no longer be driven; that he has a standard of courtesy and tactfulness far higher than our own; that an outbreak of ill-temper is a failure of nerve far more deplorable to his eyes than to ours; that what matters in the Englishman brought into association with Indians is above all the secret attitude of his spirit; is he teachable, modest, full of genuine good-will (in distinction to system-mongering); or on the other hand does he unconsciously regard his contacts with Indians as opportunities for the expression of his own dominance-drive?

If, by the grace of God, the Englishman can adopt and retain this right attitude of the spirit towards his Indian friends, he will find as the years go by that he is learning more and more from them of things quite inexpressibly important and delightful.

V

THE INDIAN VILLAGE

THERE ARE NOT far short of a million villages in India. They are extremely interesting, but extremely saddening places. They are often very picturesque; and they contain many relics of the ancient village-organization, which in normal times used to make the village an almost entirely independent and self-sufficient community, ruled by an informal council, called the *panchayat*, consisting of heads of families, each village having its own body of village craftsmen. Modern developments have, however, imposed on these ancient institutions a system of land-tenure which is often grossly unjust to the peasants, and con-currently therewith a vast swarm of parasitic money-lenders. In the old days the villagers might suffer grievously from the occasional visits of rapacious tax-gatherers, but transactions were then almost entirely in kind. The new money-economy which came in with Western civilization made possible an im-mense extension of the oppressions of landlordism and of money-lending. Therewith came also the incubus of a grow-ing fondness for going to law, at crushing expense, in connec-tion with all manner of petty village disputes.

Thus the Indian village is a saddening, and indeed distress-ing, place to live in, because of its poverty, and because of the disease which is the invariable accompaniment of deep poverty.

The team of Europeans which worked in Bihar in 1935, after the great earthquake, helping the peasants re-establish wrecked villages, found that though food-prices were about one-fourth of the corresponding prices in England, the peas-ants were not paid in cash at all for their work as agricultural labourers, but received in the case of men three tumblers-full of rice, worth about a penny-halfpenny, and in the case of women, about half that amount, for a day's work. Many of the peasant families were large, and had to be supported on this minute pittance of food. In the coldest part of the cold-weather, when ice was occasionally observed on water in the open air, these peasants had nothing in the shape of bedding, and only the thinnest cotton cloths to keep themselves warm. They could not even warm themselves by proper fires, as the only fuel was cow-dung. Their houses were merely flimsy erections of grass mats, the only furniture being a few brass pots. Their ignorance was such that it was rare to find a peasant who could count above twenty. This ignorance was found to be at the root of much of the power of the money-lenders, who in consequence of it find no difficulty in manipulating accounts to their own advantage.

About the same time an investigation in the United Provinces showed that the average agricultural holding was only four-fifths of an acre, an impossibly low amount, especially under Indian conditions, for the maintenance of a decent standard of life. The census of 1941 showed that there was a total acreage of 257,701,629 under crops in British India. The average holding for each agriculturalist in British India, in 1931, worked out at 2.9 acres, whilst per head of total population the area cropped was just about two-thirds of an acre. It is reckoned in Europe that an average of 2 ½ acres under cultivation per head of population is necessary if the land is to keep the population above the poverty line.

The 1941 census showed that under normal conditions, i.e., in the absence of acute famines, epidemics or natural disasters, the Indian population increases at a fairly steady rate of 15 per cent. for each ten years' period between the censuses.* This

* In the latest decennial period (1931–41) the Indian population increased by over 50 millions. (I am indebted to the India Office for census figures.)

means that the population of a city the size of London is now added to India every eighteen months or so. As the Indian economic system is still predominantly agricultural, and is markedly inelastic, the result of such a state of affairs (even if no other factor be taken into account) is a steady deterioration of the Indian peasantry into ever deeper destitution.

The investigation in the United Provinces already referred to showed the extreme injustice and oppression consequent upon the system of land-tenure in that and other areas. The land-owner exercises feudal rights. In the times of the Moghal Empire, before the British took over control, he was merely a tax-collector under the State; but we turned him into a permanent landlord. He has little sense of responsibility to the peasantry, and makes few improvements. Rents are excessive; 55 per cent. of them goes to the landlord, and the rest to Government in the form of land-tax. There is much trickery and petty oppression carried on by this functionless and parasitic landlord class. In very many areas the landlords are money-lenders as well as landlords, and hence have a double strangle-hold on the peasantry. It is reported on good authority that in bad years, when the Government has remitted the land-tax in part or in whole, the landlord will collect as before from the peasantry, himself keeping the amounts remitted. Oppressive feudal rights still persist, the landlord being able to call on the tenant to plough the fields of his home-farm, and to supply him with milk and grain on special occasions. The catastrophic drop in agricultural prices during the recent period of depression made the peasant's lot far harder even than before. The great majority of the peasantry are in abject poverty, few of the children can be given milk; they look like shadows, and easily fall victims to disease.* The whole system calls for urgent revision and correction. During the years of Congress Government

---

* The average income per head in India in 1930, i.e., before the depression had got well under weigh, was reckoned at 1/– per week.

from 1937 to 1939, hopeful beginnings were made in this direction.

In many parts of India the peasants get considerably less food than the prisoners in the jails, a fact which is not without its bearing on the problem of crime in rural areas.

In 1937 it was discovered that at a rural brickworks in the north of the Central Provinces women were being paid the equivalent of threepence a day for the work of carrying heavy loads of bricks on their heads. These loads often weighed 48 pounds each. Work lasted for twelve hours a day.

In 1935 the Report of the Government of India Health Commissioner gave these comparative figures of average food-consumption per head of the population:—

United Kingdom	2,400 units
India	400 to 500 units

Incidentally it is worth remembering that India pays on the average three shillings per head of her population in interest on British investments in that country. Many of these investments have repaid their principal one hundred times over or more!

Unemployment is a terrible problem in the Indian village. The agriculturalist is without work, for seasonal and climatic reasons, during some four months of the year. There is therefore grievous need for subsidiary industries, of a simple domestic character if possible, in order to give him and his family a secondary source of income. In past days these cottage industries used to exist, but they have been killed by the modern factory. It must be realized that there is no poor relief and no unemployment insurance.

The problem of unemployment is almost as acute amongst the middle class people as amongst the agriculturalists, and is not of a merely seasonal type. In a recent year, of forty-one B.A.'s graduated from a North India college only four had got jobs many months later; of these four one was receiving the equivalent of six shillings a week, two the equivalent of nine shillings and sixpence, and the fourth the equivalent of twelve shillings. They were of course regarded as amazingly fortunate to have got such jobs. In Calcutta a few years ago a subordinate post was advertised in the press carrying a salary of nine shillings and sixpence a week. There were four thousand applications for the post, from B.A.'s and M.A.'s!

With the increase of population has come another appalling problem, that of the fragmentation of holdings. A father will split his own holding, already minute, amongst his sons. This will go on till many of the fields are little bigger than a fair-sized carpet. In the year 1800 there was an average of two and a half acres of cultivated land per head of the population. To-day, as we have seen, the average is two-thirds of an acre. But it is seldom that this meagre average amount is held in one plot. The tiny fields which make up the agriculturalist's patrimony are often scattered widely asunder, and the working of them thus involves endless waste of time and labour.

Many attempts have been made, both by legislation and through cooperative action, to solve the problem of fragmentation, and to bring about the consolidation of holdings; but the process of improvement is very slow and difficult. It seems clear that to succeed, these and other needful measures of agricultural reform must be accompanied by a great increase in popular education. The present illiteracy and ignorance of the peasantry greatly increases the dead weight of custom, conservatism and lethargy, and seems often to render progress impossible.

A friend of mine recently visited the home of a student whom he had taught in College. He found the family in miserable poverty. Their total holding of land was only three acres; and yet they were in a position so greatly superior to their neighbours that it was looked upon as natural that they should aspire to have a son at college! This case illustrates another factor in the rural scene in India—where the benefits of school and college training have been appreciated, there comes into evidence an almost fanatical belief in education, and a willingness to make incredible sacrifices in order to acquire it. This tendency makes still more grave the problem of middle-class unemployment.

My friend examined the books of a money-lender, whom he found to be in the habit of lending out sums of one rupee in the morning to hawkers. The loans had to be returned the same evening, together with a sum in interest which worked out at 500 per cent. per annum. The Royal Commission on Labour in India, which went into the question of indebtedness thoroughly, regarded it as a most serious feature of the situation that debts were enforceable at law, and were held to be heritable from father to son.

When I myself was on Famine service in the North-east of the Central Provinces in 1921, it was common to see the Afghan money-lenders, great stalwart men, often no doubt with concealed arms about them, passing to and fro amongst the starving villagers, and offering them loans for the purchase of the grain which the Government was bringing in, at rates which worked out at round about 150 per cent. per annum.

The power of the money-lender is so great in the Indian village, as also in the Indian city, that a very large proportion of the population can only be described as permanently enslaved to him. In many ways the position of the money-lender's victim is worse than that of a slave; for after all it is in the interest of a slave-master to keep his property fit and healthy, both in body and mind. The Indian money-lender, whether in village or city, knows no such responsibility.

Mention has been made of the disastrous effects of the world-depression upon Indian agriculture. A very highly placed official of the British Government, in a letter to *The Times* in

1934, reckoned that the average income of the peasants of the Bombay Presidency was in that year only two-fifths of what it had been before the slump. There has been some measure of recovery since then; but the fact remains that the poor are steadily becoming poorer. Even primary school teachers in rural parts of Bengal are often paid only one shilling and four-pence a week. In Cawnpore it was reported a few years ago that domestic servants were paid one shilling a week (without keep), and that the municipal scavengers were receiving from two shillings to three shillings and ninepence per week.

An investigator in a rural area of Bihar, a few years back, went into the budget of a typical low-caste family. He found them living in a hut measuring 10 feet in length, 6 feet in breadth, and 3 feet 6 inches in height. There were four members of the family. They possessed no furniture or bedding except a few cooking vessels. The father earned an average of twopence a day for six months of the year. The rest of the time he was unemployed. The total income of the family worked out at the equivalent of 34/6 per annum, the price of rice being then about three farthings a pound. In English values this means that they were trying to live on an expenditure of about two shillings each per month.*

With poverty so wide-spread and deeply rooted, it is inevi-table that disease will take a frightful toll of the Indian village population. In the pneumonia epidemic of 1918 the deaths in India exceeded all the war deaths of all the belligerent nations of the 1914–18 war put together. Even in ordinary years malaria, cholera, dysentery and other diseases kill innumerable Indian villagers. There are several million lepers.

Yet there are hopeful signs. The Cooperative Societies are already working a revolutionary change in many thousands of

* The report of the Directors of Public Health and Agriculture for the Madras Presidency, for 1934, showed that the average income in wages for a whole family in that Province ranged between 37/6 and 90/– per annum.

villages, especially in the North-west, and are reviving the lapsed community-spirit of the ancient Indian village. The rate they charge for the agricultural loans, which are periodically essential under present conditions, is 12½ per cent. per annum, instead of the fantastic rates charged by money-lenders, which range up to 500 per cent. One of the most encouraging features of the Cooperative movement is that it is almost entirely in Indian hands.

VI

THE INDIAN CITY

ARTEMUS WARD used to say that the distinguishing feature about George Washington was that there is nobody like him to-day. The same might be said of the ruined cities of India, for example, the great Emperor Akbar's capital at Fatehpur Sikri in the North, with its predominantly Islamic architecture, and the deserted Hindu capital Vijayanagar in the South. Both cities are built of a lovely rose-coloured stone. Both give to the visitor who wanders through their deserted streets, and examines the wonderful sculpture in palaces and shrines, a sense of the power and magnificence of ancient India. He cannot however help comparing these impressions with the reality as he knows it of life in modern Indian cities, where the poverty and wretchedness of the common people is even more apparent than in the villages.

Many casual visitors to India see only what are called the "Civil Stations"—pleasant garden-cities, with fine modern buildings, ample space, and many gardens and parks—which have been created well outside the big Indian centres of population, as safe and agreeable places of residence for European officials. The true Indian city is a very different place from the "Civil Station," though the two may lie close together. In the former, population is congested to a point scarcely conceivable to us in the West. In Bombay, for instance, it is not at all exceptional for fifteen people to occupy a single room. This means that they merely use it as a place in which to do a little cooking, on a minute brazier, and to keep a box for the very few family belongings, generally limited to cooking vessels. The families actually sleep in passages, lanes or streets, alongside the walls, and under the feet of pedestrians and wandering cattle. This may sound incredible to Westerners, but anyone who has seen a big Indian city at night, especially a city like Bombay, will know that it is true.

In consequence of this terrible congestion of population the average Indian city, except as regards its main streets, is generally a place of indescribable filth and smells. Though great progress has been made in the introduction of modern methods of sanitation, the ignorance of the people and the manner in which they are herded together render anything like Western standards of cleanliness unattainable.

In every city there are also appalling slum areas, often inhabited by Outcastes and Untouchables, where the flimsiness of the huts, the pungency of the smells and the appalling filth remind the visitor who has been intrepid enough to penetrate to such purlieus that they are the breeding-places of all manner of disastrous epidemic diseases.

All this is illustration of the fact that poverty in India is becoming deeper and deeper and more and more widespread. As the population increases, in an unelastic rural economy, life in the villages becomes impossible for fresh hundreds of thousands of people every year. They hear tales from the cities of higher rates of pay than they have ever dreamt possible. They do not realize that living expenses in the cities, even for the poorest of the poor, are very much higher than in the village. Thus they drift to the city, destined to become the debt-slaves of city money-lenders and labour-jobbers.

The fate of these destitute slum-dwellers in the big cities is far more heart-rending than the fate of the destitute villagers. The latter at least starve in their own home-environment. They may have an infinitesimal stake left in the world, in the form of a tiny field, inalienable however deeply mortgaged, and therefore in a sense their own. They are amongst neighbours and friends whom they have known from their childhood. The caste-organization of village society means that if the worst comes to the worst, they have people in their close neighbourhood from whom they have a right to try to beg a crust before they actually starve.

But once they come to the city, everything is different. They are dismayed by the noise of the traffic, the hurry and bustle, the height of the buildings, above all the heartless unneighbourliness of everyone around them. They are terribly alone. They have no root in the body politic, no anchorage on the land, no stake in the vast and complicated economy in the midst of which they find themselves. The caste-sanctions of conduct break down. Various types of demoralization consequently appear, in an acute form. There is no reason to keep traditional rules of cleanliness, either in personal habits or in moral conduct. Consequently the slums of these great cities become sinks of corruption, both in outward conditions and as regards the morality of the slum-dwellers.

Above all there are the inhuman conditions of their labour in the great factories (if they are lucky enough to get a job), and the tyranny of the exploitation under which they groan, both as mill-hands and as debt-slaves to money-lender and jobber.

A very sinister element in the life of the Indian city is the tendency to strife, often bloody strife, between Hindu and Moslem. In the country districts there is little such strife; but under the nerve-racking and unnatural conditions of the Indian industrial city tempers wear thin and riots and fighting easily break out. The big industrial city in which I was living in 1927 was for three days in the hands of a Hindu mob, which knocked on the head any Moslem caught in the streets. In 1924 what looked like the outbreak of a general civil war between the two communities was averted by Mr. Gandhi's fast of that year, a fast which succeeded in creating a new spirit of good-will. That good-will was worn thin enough on various occasions since 1924 to allow of the sporadic outbreak of fresh conflicts; but there has always been present in the background a knowledge that a way does exist by which hostility may be changed into fellowship, and that Mr. Gandhi followed that way in 1924.

One of the main causes of Hindu-Moslem hatred is the existence of the pernicious system of separate communal electorates, which came into play in the epoch of the beginnings of Indian democracy, before the last war, and has been perpetuated in constitutional reforms ever since. Under this arrangement, since only Moslems vote for Moslem members of the legislatures, and Hindus for Hindus, it is only the communally-conscious and embittered Moslems and Hindus that have a chance of getting elected; and they get elected by fomenting communal differences and disagreements, so as to give the voters the impression that the communal candidate has "ginger" in him, and will stand up for communal rights. The consequence is a steady deterioration of communal relationships.

Instead of these communal electorates, in which the seeds of war are so obviously present, Mr. Gandhi desires big multi-member constituencies, with reservation of seats for the several communities. Thus a city (and surrounding district) of a million people might return, say, three members to the central federal legislature and twelve to the provincial legislature. Instead of (as at present) letting all the Moslems vote for one Moslem member, and all the Hindus for two Hindu members of the federal legislature; and all the Moslems vote for four Moslem members, all the Hindus for seven Hindu members, and all the Parsis (say) for one Parsi member, of the provincial legislature, Mr. Gandhi would have everyone vote for one Moslem and two Hindus, in the former case, and for four Moslems, seven Hindus and one Parsi, in the latter. By this means it would be only moderate men, tolerant and courteous towards the other community, who would have a chance of being elected; for a fierce Moslem fanatic would never gain Hindu votes, and vice-versa. Thus in process of time an active principle of reconciliation would be brought into play at the federal and provincial elections, instead of the present dangerously increasing bitterness and hostility.

This matter is not just an affair of electoral machinery. The bringing of peace between the two great communities means a scrupulously careful watch against occasions of ill-will; and under the existing system this business of elections presents one of the most menacing of such occasions of ill-will.

The populace of the typical Indian city is politically exceedingly inflammable. It is not only in connection with the communal problem, just mentioned, that fierce rioting is apt to break out at a moment's notice. The arrest of a well-known political leader, or the rumour of such an arrest, a so-called "insult" to the national flag, a politically-engineered general strike (these are common), or a hundred and one other incidents may become inexplicably the signal for the assembly of vast and angry crowds, and the outbreak of mob-violence, often directed against the (extremely unpopular) police.

A really excited crowd in India is an awesome thing. But it has a better side, to which appeal can be made. On two occasions friends and colleagues of mine have been caught by such crowds, and have apparently been in imminent danger of lynching, on account of their complexion. On the first occasion, the Scotchman in question, who was on his bicycle, and had ridden unexpectedly round a corner into the leading sections of an excited crowd, saved the situation and probably his own life, by taking off his hat and waving it in a comic manner (he was an adept at such things). The crowd's sense of humour was tickled; and its front ranks broke into a shout of laughter. Tension was immediately relaxed, with very practical advantages to everyone concerned.

On the other occasion it was an old Scottish lady, riding in a bullock-carriage, who was in the situation of danger. She also made friends with the leading files of the crowd which had unexpectedly surrounded her, by smiling, waving her hand, and cracking a joke or two in their own language. Tension was relaxed and the situation saved.

These two instances are not trivial. They stand for the fact that in every Indian crowd, as in every Indian individual, there is something to which appeal can be made, if only the right fashion can be discovered of making that appeal. In the two cases just given it was friendly humour that made the successful advance. Sometimes it is merely readiness to listen courteously to grievances, and tact in finding a means of redress. More subtly it is often entirely an affair of psychological attitude, the friendliness of the manner (for instance) in which quite trifling and banal observations are made, or the teachableness and humility of the way in which quite outrageous suggestions are received and, instead of being derided, are analysed and shown up, in a spirit of temperate reasonableness, for what they are really worth.

The thronging streets of a true Indian city are extraordinarily interesting and picturesque. I used during one part of my time in India to cycle several miles every day through such streets. They were narrow, and smelly. Progress was continually blocked by drivers of bullock-carts who knew nothing and cared less for the rule of the road, and by long lines of villagers bringing market-produce into the town in huge baskets, or firewood in great long bundles, balanced on their heads. Immense cotton-carts bringing raw materials to the mills were a more serious obstacle. Every now and then one would be held up by a wedding-procession, in glorious array; or by a body of scantily clothed mourners singing sorrowfully as they escorted the body of a dead friend towards the burning-ghat. At the sides of the streets were open shops filled with brassware or bales of cloth, foodstuffs or sweetmeats, according to the locality. Every now and then one had to give way respectfully before the majestic advance of a huge sacred bull.

But this was in a city where much of the old India is still left. The main streets of the great modern centres of population, especially Calcutta and Bombay, are anything but like this. They are crowded with motor traffic, and from the human point of view show much more deplorable evidence of the destitution of the Indian urban proletariat.

Every few years there is a plague alarm. Rats begin dying, and are found to be infected; and then, at least in the case of cities still genuinely Indian, there is a general movement of evacuation. In a day or two a whole quarter, perhaps even the whole city, will become deserted; and somewhere, perhaps several miles away, in the open country outside, a huge array of temporary shacks, of all degrees of ramshackleness, will have sprung up. The children enjoy these exoduses immensely; but not so their parents!

An abiding memory of Indian city life is the sound of the temple bells, and the sight of worshippers on their way, with offerings of flowers. There are other signs of the vitality of Indian religion. Not far from the gates of a great modern cotton-mill, in the city where I lived, an old Hindu ascetic sat, in a quiet spot near a large pool of water. In the pursuit of Absolute Truth he had felt it his duty to hold his arms above his head, for thirty years. They were shrivelled into thin sticks, and entirely immovable. The nails had grown through the palms (the hands were clasped). But still he held his arms above his head, in his soul's search for Release.

The census of 1941 in India showed a total increase of over fifty millions on 1931, or 15 per cent. in ten years. The Hindus numbered roughly 255 millions, the Moslems 94 millions, the Christians 7¼ millions, the Sikhs 6 millions, the Parsis only 115,000. One sinister aspect of the census returns was the fact that in India there are twelve million more males than females, whereas in the West there is usually a preponderance the other way. The main reason for this can be nothing but the stress of economic conditions, which make a daughter a liability rather than an asset (especially in view of dowry conditions and the prevailing costliness of wedding-festivities), so that she is less carefully looked after than a boy. In addition there is the heavy maternal mortality, due to primitive health-services and to prevailing superstitions and prejudices. It is a disquieting fact that the discrepancy between the numbers of males and females is increasing; in 1931 it was 51.55 per cent. males, in 1941 51.68 per cent. The reason is almost certainly the increasing economic strain due to the fast growing population.

The cropped acreage in 1941 was 258 million acres, which is about two-thirds of an acre per head of the population, whereas in the West in a mainly agricultural economy two and a half acres per head is reckoned the minimum on which a population can be kept above the poverty line. These figures also are full of menace.

The most encouraging feature of the census-returns is the increase in literacy, which has gone up from 7 per cent. in 1931 to 12 per cent. in 1941. In the Bombay Presidency there was a 100 per cent. increase. Much of the credit for this improvement must go to the Congress Governments which took over Education in several of the largest Provinces between 1937 and 1939; and to other Indian Ministries in the rest of the Provinces. Obviously however there must be no spirit of contentment with an 88 per cent. illiteracy still to combat, and with such discouragements to face as the fact that 72 per cent. of the pupils entering Primary School fail to reach literacy, being withdrawn by their parents before they can do so, for economic reasons, largely connected with the herding of cattle.

The most striking fact of all in regard to the census of 1941 is the extraordinary growth in the population of the big cities. Calcutta has grown by 85 per cent., from 1,411,000 to 2,109,-

000 in the ten years, and is now the largest city in India, having outstripped Bombay, which only increased by 28 per cent., to about a million and a half. Cawnpore has doubled in population. Ahmedabad has nearly doubled. Jamshedpur has increased 77 per cent., and ten other large towns over 50 per cent. These figures mean that a "rush to the cities" is taking place on an unprecedented scale. In consequence the living-conditions for the mass of the city-population in the slums which lie every-where, behind the facade of a few fine streets, are becoming more and more appallingly congested.

As we have seen, these slum-dwellers are uprooted from all the old sanctions and the traditional moralities of village-life. In the city they have no position in the community, as they have had in the village, however poor they may have been. They lose heart, become enslaved to money-lenders, fall ill. The Royal Commission on Indian Labour found in 1929 that the average life in health of a Bombay mill-hand was only ten months. Their misery when they fall ill, under such living-conditions, may be better imagined than described.

Hence the swift growth of great industrial cities in India, in spite of gallant efforts to improve conditions, is a dreadful menace to human happiness and welfare.

There is however another side to this matter. The mill-hands often belong to the depressed and Untouchable classes. In the villages they are scattered, and always in a small minor-ity as compared with the caste Hindus, perhaps only four or five families out of a village containing thirty families in all. There are other outcastes in neighbouring villages; but there, too, they are in a minority. Here in the city, on the other hand, the Outcastes live close together, thousands upon thousands of them; and in the districts where they live other sections of the population are in a very small minority. Consequently they are becoming conscious of their power, both as workers who may strike, and as voters who at any rate in some local elections, where the franchise is very wide, may make their influence felt. In Provincial elections also, there are special arrangements for the representation of the Outcastes, and in practice this means chiefly the city-Outcastes, since they are the only section of the outcaste community vocal and conscious of their position, their rights and their needs. Hence in the modern industrial city, grisly as the conditions of their life are, the Outcastes are getting to know and to use their power. That fact is big with meaning for the future in India.

VII

THE INDIAN INDUSTRIAL WORKER

INDIA IS THE eighth industrial country of the world. She is reckoned to have about 7 per cent. of her population, i.e., well over 26,000,000 people, dependent upon industry of one kind and another. Wages vary greatly, but are often grotesquely small. They are nearly always entirely inadequate for the support of a family above the poverty line.

As we have seen, pressure of population in rural districts, and the decay of village industries, drive the country people in increasing numbers into the industrial towns, so that many of these towns have increased from 50 to 100 per cent. during the last decennial period between the censuses. It is a common sight to see wandering up and down the streets of such cities, with an expression of blank hopelessness and helplessness on their faces, the most recent arrivals from the country districts. They are looking for work, for places to live, for food. Such people fall inevitably into the hands of rapacious money-lenders who give them loans at extortionate rates to tide over the first period of their arrival in the city. As they have no sort of security to offer (whereas the villager in his relations with the money-lender has a certain position in the community), these new-comers have to pay in interest any rate, however extortionate, that the money-lender likes to demand. It is hard to exaggerate the pitiableness of their position.

In time the immigrant from the countryside will get into touch with a labour-jobber, who will have to be bribed in order to get him a job. More loans will be needful to supply the bribe. The jobber is probably a money-lender himself, and offers an advance of pay, again at extortionate rates of interest, for the purchase of equipment, tools, etc., and for the provision of rent and other household expenses. The villager, being entirely unlettered, has no means of knowing how cruelly he is fleeced in the calculation of the interest on these debts, and in other ways. Even after he has started work, he may have to wait seven weeks for his first pay, since pay-day comes only once a month, and the mills keep three weeks back-pay in hand in order to prevent his running away! By the end of these first seven weeks the villager is in very many cases already hopelessly and permanently in debt, both to the money-lender (who will often be a particularly large and muscular Pathan from across the North-west frontier) and to the jobber. In any industrial city it is common to see, on pay-day, the money-lenders lined up in a formidable array outside the mill-gates, ready to pounce on their wretched "clients" as they come out, and to take from them every penny of their pay that the jobber has spared. For the coming month the money-lender merely allows the mill-hand the wretched modicum of inferior rice to keep him and his family alive.

Under such conditions it is not to be wondered at that the Indian mill-hand lives a life of almost undiluted destitution and misery. In a case well known to myself a worker had incurred a debt of the equivalent of about four pounds. I got an actuary to inquire into the rate of interest being charged, and the eventual result. If the man could pay none back, which was extremely likely owing to the smallness of his pay, the size of his family, and the manner in which the money-lenders keep their accounts, the debt in a few years' time would amount to the equivalent not of four pounds, but of four thousand pounds! In other words the man had plunged into a bottom-less bog, in which he would wallow for the rest of his life. His sons would wallow there too, for unfortunately these debts are handed on from father to son, and it is regarded as a matter of family honour to keep on trying to pay them.

Under such conditions we need not wonder that the Indian mill-hand cannot spend much on rent. A recent investigation discovered that 97 per cent. of the population of Bombay were living in one room tenements, or in less than one room. Where such congestion exists, disease is rife. It used to be regarded as almost equivalent to a sentence of death for a teacher to be sent down from the Central Province to Bombay for further training, because the risk was so great of his developing tuberculosis in the crowded quarters of the city where alone he would be able to get accommodation. The Royal Commission on Labour in India came to the conclusion in 1929 that the village-immigrant to the city breaks down in health on the average after ten months of work only. He then either drags on in misery till he dies, or returns to his village, carrying disease with him and the fear that the money-lender and the jobber, or their agents, will follow and catch him even there!

To quote from the Royal Commission's Report:—"We are satisfied that the majority of Indian workers are in debt for the greater part of their lives. Many indeed are born in debt, and it evokes both admiration and regret to find how commonly a son assumes responsibility for his father's debt. In a number of cases a stage is reached when the money-lender takes from the worker the whole of his wages, paying him only sufficient for subsistence, and even puts the members of the worker's family to work on a similar basis. Whatever the figure of actual payment, the result is almost invariable; the indebted worker has to give all of what might otherwise be his savings to the money-lender, and these payments are not merely the surplus that would be spent on petty luxuries; they have often to be provided by trenching on the primary needs of a healthy life."

If the Commissioners had been a little more acquainted with the realities of Indian industrial life they would not have thought it worth while to put in those words about "petty luxuries!"

Margaret Read's excellent book, *The Indian Peasant Uprooted*, which deals with the findings of this same Royal Commission on Indian Labour, makes the following additional comment at this point:—"The Pathan (money-lender) and his swaggering ruffians brandishing their *lathis* (brass-bound clubs) beset the mill-gates on pay-day, or follow their victims to the chawls or bustis (slums) and there deal summarily with them. A threat of violence may be enough to extort some payment of the interest due. If threats do not avail the lathi with its leaded end is laid about the shoulders of the wretched man till he hands over some of his earnings." Often, as the Commission Report points out, it is the whole of those earnings. "In some mills the money-lender even stands by the pay-desk and receives his interest on the spot. Again he may receive an attachment of wages in a law-court and so pocket the whole of the worker's wages."

It will be seen that industrial slavery is a genuine and actual thing in India.

One of the chief obstacles in the way of all attempts to break the vicious circle of such slavery is the ignorance of the mill-hands. It is entirely impossible for completely unlettered workers either to organize themselves in order to obtain labour rights from the mill managements, as regards pay and hours of work, etc., or to resist the oppression of jobbers and money-lenders. Many attempts, some of them more successful than others, have been made in the industrial cities to meet this need by the provision of night-schools, especially for the younger mill-hands. It has been found in practice, however, that the vast majority of them are so exhausted by their long hours of labour in the heat and stuffiness of the mills, that they have not the vitality left to derive much profit from the night-school. Still, if all that can be done is to give the young worker an elementary knowledge of arithmetic, so that he may keep some sort of check on the money-lender's accounts, this will be a great boon to him.

Child-labour is illegal in India, and energetic efforts have been made by the authorities to get the regulations against it enforced. But this is an extremely difficult enterprise. The offence is generally committed in the smaller factories of the less important industrial towns. The Factory Inspector may take elaborate precautions, in order to keep his visit secret. In one case, known to myself, the Inspector took the trouble to take a motor-bicycle with him on his visit of inspection to a suspected area. He got off the train at a station some way back, mounted his bicycle, and rode as fast as he could to the small industrial town where he believed abuses of the child-labour regulations were taking place. It was impossible that news of his visit could have got about, as he had told no one that he was intending to make it! None the less, as he raced into the town, he saw signals being given, and as he drew up at the factory-gates, after an exciting navigation of the streets, the last of the children were disappearing over the walls round the mill compound!

It is probable that large numbers of children, down to the age of five, are worked for twelve hours a day in factories in remote places.* Even in the more important centres attempts to introduce half-time work for children of certain ages have merely resulted in their working half the day in one factory and the other half in another. With economic conditions such as they are for the workers it is difficult to see how such attempts to get extra income for the industrial family can be avoided.

We have noticed how seriously caste-standards of morality are apt to break down in the Indian industrial city, where the ex-villager feels himself completely uprooted from all that used

---

* And adult workers, it is to be feared, are often worked for 18 hours continuously.

to bind him to life. Wholesale prostitution is perhaps the most serious symptom of this breakdown. In Calcutta, for instance, the Royal Commission found that in one district one in three of the women mill-hands admitted to being prostitutes, and in another district one in four.

Again, there is the problem of infant mortality in the slum areas. In Bombay in 1921 the vital statistics showed that 672 per thousand of children born died within the first year of life. These figures contrasted with a ratio of 178 per thousand for the Bombay Presidency as a whole. This shows how dangerous to the physical well-being of the people is life in an industrial city. Very considerable improvement has been made during recent years in health services in Bombay, and the infantile mortality rate is now greatly reduced: but the main fact continues true—life in an Indian industrial city automatically condemns to death an extremely high percentage of the young children.

A flagrant abuse in mill-management is the fines system, which the Royal Commission found to be almost universal. For trivial offences heartlessly big cuts are made from wages already disastrously insufficient.

One ward in Bombay has 500 people to the acre, as was established by a recent investigation. This will show what congestion is like in Indian slums. The average for London is 60 per acre. I was recently told by a professor who had been resident in Cawnpore that one of the wards in that city has a population-density of nearly one thousand per acre. The Bombay investigation just quoted showed 135 cases where a single room was shared by six families or more, and came to the conclusion that the infantile mortality of families living in one room or sharing a single room is more than twice as high as that in other cases.

Conditions are especially bad in the coal-mines. The Royal Commission found the mining families living in houses built back to back, without provision for lighting. Cooking was done over a kerosine stove. There was no sanitary accommodation except the open fields, and the water supply was entirely inadequate. The morning meal was usually taken at eight a.m. and consisted of rice and salt and nothing else. The evening meal was taken when the workers came out of the mine (an indefinite time, for the Commission found cases of workers remaining underground for 20 or even 36 hours). It consisted of rice only. What such a diet means for workers engaged on the exceedingly heavy labour in coal-mines may be imagined.

One of the most essential workers in India is the municipal sweeper or scavenger. On his faithfulness depends the health of the whole community. Yet he is an outcaste, and often has an especially hard lot. In a town in Bengal the sweepers were recently found to be paying 225 per cent. interest on money-lenders' loans. In a town in the United Provinces their wages were found to average under three shillings a week. In Ajmere unspeakably disgusting conditions of work, involving great danger to health, were found to be imposed upon them. These are but isolated instances showing that this most essential of all types of labour receives a peculiarly raw deal under existing conditions in India.

Yet there are elements of hope in the industrial situation. In spite of the acute sufferings of the depression period the report of the Royal Commission of 1929 brought about certain reforms; so did the Congress governments of 1937-9. The horrors of women's labour in coal-mines have been brought to a stop, although in other types of industry it is probably still true that women are not infrequently worked for 24 hours on end. The workers, in spite of their ignorance, are slowly becoming more conscious of their numbers and of their powers. They are developing leadership of their own, and are beginning to organize themselves. Education is spreading amongst them. Large numbers of them are Untouchables; and Mr. Gandhi's movement for the uplift of the "Harijans" ("children of God," his name for the Untouchables) has begun to affect them favourably. So also has the movement for the organization of the outcastes led by Dr. Ambedkar. Especially in Bihar during the period of Congress government valiant efforts have been made to curb the power of money-lenders. In Bombay and elsewhere much has been done to check drunkenness.

Progress is slow, but it exists.

VIII

THE CASTE SYSTEM

WE HAVE NOTICED already that caste originated in a colour-bar, and continued in the stratification of ancient Indian society into four main hereditary classes, each of which had a different function to perform in the community. These four main classes have become divided and sub-divided until there are now thousands of castes. The great majority of these still have an economic basis, their members performing certain definite services for the community.

It is common for Westerners to see nothing but evil in the caste-system. It will be of advantage therefore to find out at once what good things are to be discerned in it.

In the first place, the caste-system has a certain efficacy in guarding against starvation and acute unemployment, especially in rural areas which are still economically at a somewhat primitive level. As each caste has its own trade, each member of a caste learns to practise that trade and in times of unemployment may expect to have at any rate a certain amount of work to do for the community. If he cannot obtain work in his own caste-line in his home-area, he may be able to obtain it elsewhere, at some place where there happens to be a dearth of workers in his craft.

Like the mediaeval guild-system in Europe the caste-system also provides a rough-and-ready means of keeping up standards of handicraft, regulating prices, preventing cornering of commodities, and so forth. In big modern centres of population the system will of course not be able to perform these functions properly; but this does not alter the fact that elsewhere, and over the vastly greater part of India, conditions are so simple economically that the caste-system still fulfils useful economic functions.

In the second place, caste began as a method of enabling two or more racially distinct communities to live peacefully together on the same territory. Under primitive conditions each caste was to a considerable degree a little *imperium in imperio*. It was in each locality self-governing as regards internal affairs (and some external affairs also), the heads of the chief caste-families administering a rude justice and forming a council for the direction of communal affairs. Whenever necessary, and especially at the times when the state-government collected its taxes, this caste-council served as a body through whom negotiations and arrangements could be made. The hierarchy of various castes in any given locality with their caste-councils formed in fact a kind of primitive "federal union" in that locality.

Again through the existence of the caste-organization of society the members of conquered races were saved from extermination, and were given a definite place and function in the body politic. It is not for us Westerners to be over-critical of such achievements or of the means through which they were made possible. The Anglo-Saxon conquest of England was probably accompanied by something like the extermination of the British population over large areas of the country; but the existence of the caste-system seems to have saved India from such blood-baths (at any rate till the coming of the Moslems), though conquests and re-conquests have been almost innumerable. This is no small matter to be reckoned to the credit of the caste-system.

Again, over long periods of Indian history, the caste-system has prevented the emergence of a class-problem of Western lines. Though there has been exploitation by great land-owners from time immemorial, the tremendous strength of the caste-organization in the economic field has prevented industrial exploitation developing to anything like a formidable degree, till the arrival of Western industrialism began that shattering of caste which we have already noticed. In the small-scale industry of the country-town masters and men were not only working together, as in mediaeval Europe, in one household economy. They were also bound together by caste-allegiance, caste-ethics, caste-interests. It must be realized that the whole caste-system arose under the aegis of religion, and continues to exist only under the aegis of religion. Long before the time of Gautama Buddha India was being taught that the right observance of caste-duties and caste-ceremonial is a main Way of Release from the weary wheel of existence. Much later, when the *Gita*, the "New Testament of the Hindus" was written, the author of that transcendently important and transcendently beautiful book laid it down authoritatively that the Way of Release is Devotion to a personal Saviour-God (Krishna in the *Gita*), together with the right performing of caste-duty, in the atmosphere of that devotion, and in service to the community.

To the average Hindu, even to-day, this authority is final. He performs unquestioningly his caste-ceremonial and works at his caste-trade, both alike in the spirit of religious devotion: and he serves God in performing honestly and well his caste-function for the community in which he is set.

These are high values for a social system to attain, and important functions for it to perform. They must be recognized honestly before the caste-system is light-heartedly condemned. Furthermore, those who propose to do away with caste wholesale must be first provided with something else to put in its place. As we have noticed, the condition of demoralization into which villagers fall on reaching the cities to become industrial workers shows quite clearly that caste-sanctions have a definite value, and that their indiscriminate destruction leads to disaster.

Mr. Gandhi, whose attitude on such questions is of the highest importance, does not approve of any design for the total and immediate ending of the caste-system. He believes that it should be reformed and purged of its abuses, not by revolutionary action in the ordinary sense, but by slow and patient advance towards all-India brotherhood. He concentrates his efforts especially on the removal of Untouchability, the barrier between the Hindus of the great Aryan castes and the fifty millions of Outcastes below them. He believes that as India is taught to treat these Untouchables as human beings, the rigid and anti-social elements in the caste-system as a whole will give way, whilst the main benefits of the system will not be destroyed.

The crucial point in the history of Mr. Gandhi's campaign against Untouchability was probably the series of events which a number of years ago led up to the opening to the Untouchables of a certain sacred street at Vaikom, a small town in an Indian State in Southern India. The story is well known, but is so clear an illustration of Mr. Gandhi's methods that it may well be repeated once more. As is common in the South, the street in question was forbidden to Untouchables because it led up to a temple, and because Brahmins inhabited the houses on both sides of it. On a certain date the local Untouchables decided to assert their right to be treated as full human beings, by conducting a procession up the street to the temple. The procession was forbidden by the State authorities. The Untouchables persisted, held the procession, and were jailed. More and more came, and were jailed. The matter attracted wide attention, and there were thousands of outcaste volunteers available. Soon the State jails were full: and the authorities altered their tactics, throwing a cordon of police across the end of the street. The matter was referred to

Mr. Gandhi. His advice came, that the Untouchables must be unflinchingly persevering, at whatever cost, in the assertion of their rights; but that they must be entirely non-violent. They must remain up against the police cordon till it gave way.

The Untouchables obeyed. Relays of volunteers were organized. A large camp was established outside the town; and the volunteers remained pressed up against the police cordon, with their heads bowed and their hands joined in the Indian attitude of prayer, for sixteen months. The rains came, the street was flooded, the police took to boats, but the volunteers stood in deep water. There was a cholera epidemic in the camp, and many died. But they did not give way; and at last, in response to their unwearying *Satyagraha* (Mr. Gandhi's name for this type of passive resistance, meaning stalwart allegiance to truth), the State authorities yielded, and the procession of Untouchables marched in triumph up the street.

The Vaikom incident was a test case; and has led in many parts of India to movements for the emancipation of the Untouchables. Temples, schools, streets, wells and all manner of public buildings have been thrown open to them; and their treatment has in many respects greatly improved.

As we have noticed, the Untouchables are also coming somewhat slowly to realize their tremendous corporate power as industrial workers. The first section of them to come to this realization were the municipal sweepers in the big cities, whose services are absolutely essential to the health of the community. Strikes began to break out amongst these sweepers many years ago. Such strikes are declared illegal; but the fact that they had occurred and that they had perforce been taken very seriously by the authorities led to a gradual realization by the sweepers, and later by other Outcaste communities, of the powers which they possess.

In a sense lower than even the Untouchables, because of the terrible nature of the disease from which they suffer, are the lepers. Medical science has now discovered a method of treating leprosy which is almost certain to arrest the disease if the treatment is begun early enough. But even though this is so, it is often difficult to persuade lepers to submit to the treatment, not merely because it is tedious and painful, but also because of the extraordinary position of liberty and in a sense of power which his disease gives a leper. He is a highly successful beggar, if only because people are so afraid that he will touch them if they do not give to him; and for similar reasons he can obtain a free passage on the railway! He is Untouchable, loathsomely so, but he is still free and still powerful. He feels himself, even in the midst of his disease, a being of consequence.

The darkest aspect of caste, apart from Untouchability, is the position of women. As is well known, there are thousands of girl-widows in India, many of them very young indeed, who have been condemned to the life of privation and suffering, which is the traditional lot of the Hindu widow, for no fault of their own, but because caste conservatism demands that they should be punished in this way for hypothetical sins in a past existence, which sins are supposed to have brought ill luck upon the deceased husband.* One solution of this problem is obviously to be found in the prevention of child-marriage; but this is a reform easier to talk over, and even to legislate about, than to carry into effect. It is a good many years now since a bill was passed through the All India Legislature to prevent child-marriage; but the weight of social custom, especially in the South, is so heavy and oppressive that it is very doubtful whether progress in the direction of reform has been really effective.

---

* In 1931 there were 26 million widows in India, nearly 31,000 of them being under the age of five.

A slower but more sure method of preventing child-marriage is to press forward with the education of women; and not to be content with a smattering of the three R's, but to carry more and more girl-students on to secondary and higher education, so that there may be a steady supply of effective feminine leadership behind all the efforts for reform.

Another of the woes of Indian womanhood is the institution of the *purda*, or veil, especially in North India. The seclusion of women probably originated at the time of the Moslem conquests, when it was not safe for them to be seen on the public streets. The customs of the conquering Moslems probably had a direct effect also in stimulating Hindu imitation. But however it originated, the institution of *purda* now constitutes a gigantic evil. From the age of twelve or thirteen the girl is condemned to sit in seclusion at home, or if she goes abroad to wear a huge shapeless extinguisher-like covering, which hides head and face as well as body, and has only holes for seeing and breathing through. Under such conditions the women cannot but remain ignorant and narrow-minded. They take their revenge by becoming absolute and unchallenged autocrats in their own sphere, the home. This is one of the main reasons why progress is so slow in India towards social emancipation. The attitude of the older women, who are all-powerful in the home, towards proposals to educate and emancipate the girls, is too often one of jealous repression; and they succeed in imposing their point of view upon the menfolk, in regard not only to this reform but to many others, for example the combating of Untouchability.

Mr. Gandhi, many years ago, welcomed for conscience' sake an Untouchable child into his own home-life, even though at first the revolutionary step almost tore his home asunder. At public meetings to which he is invited, if (as sometimes happens even now) a separate space is set apart for the Untouchables, he will insist on coming down from the platform and taking up his position in that space, among his brethren, the Harijans, the "people of God." His example is working wonders. Many other factors are also cooperating for the lowering of caste-barriers and the loosening of caste-restrictions. Amongst them may be mentioned railway travel, in which men of many castes are crowded (often very tightly crowded) into the same compartments, inter-dining at school and college hostels (with regard to this, occasionally parents or priests make complaints and large numbers of plates which have been used for such purposes have to be smashed!), the general progress of education and enlightenment, the share taken by women in recent political movements, the Indian equivalent of women's institutes, foreign travel, etc. But the way of self-identification with the Untouchables, so practically demonstrated by Mr. Gandhi, is the most important of all.

IX

THE OUTCASTES

WE HAVE SAID a good deal already about the Outcastes; but a great deal more remains to be said. The first thing to recognize is that here is a mass of some fifty million of our fellow-citizens in the British Commonwealth who by immemorial social and religious sanctions are denied the elementary rights of human beings. Economically they are condemned to a miserable existence as village serfs, or as scavengers in the towns. They can only gain a livelihood through performing functions of an indescribably disgusting nature, which often involve close personal contact all day long with human filth. The only food they can get is often what others would regard as carrion. Worse still are their psychological sufferings, the knowledge that the great mass of their fellow-countrymen look upon them as defiling, and the permanent condition of fear which such an environment imposes upon them.

C. F. Andrews was on one occasion in a remote district of Southern India, engaged in relief work. He was dressed, as was his usual custom, in Indian dress. He became thirsty, and seeing a hut near the road, entered it to ask for a drink of water. There was only one woman in the hut, and she set up a heart-rending shriek of fear and despair. At first C. F. Andrews could not imagine what was wrong with her. Later he discovered that this was the house of an Outcaste family. Seeing this tall stranger enter her door, the woman thought that he must be a high-caste Hindu who did not know that theirs was an Untouchable family. Therefore, although she had had no responsibility at all in the matter, she and her family would be punished with cruel beatings from the caste Hindus of the locality for having brought defilement upon the visitor.

This small incident was a revelation to C. F. Andrews regarding the general state of inhuman fear in which the Outcastes in the South pass their lives. He became convinced that one of the most clamant needs in India is the doing of justice to the Untouchables; and he threw himself into the campaign to that end which Mr. Gandhi was already organizing.

The traditional attitude to the Outcastes may be gauged by the fact that in some parts of India up to not much more than a hundred years ago they were compelled to carry a pot slung round the neck, in order that if they needed to spit they might not defile the surface of the earth: and to drag behind them the branch of a tree, in order that their unhallowed foot-prints might be swept from the paths.

In the pneumonia epidemic of 1918 I remember visiting with medicines and relief a village where the land-owner was a high-caste Hindu. In the upper caste part of the village he came round with me from house to house, and showed himself very helpful and full of good-will. Then I crossed the broad stretch of ground which separated this part from the group of wretched hovels occupied by the Outcastes. The land-owner waited till I had visited all the houses in this quarter of the village. As I came back I had with me a group of Outcaste heads of families, to whom I was giving advice on diet. Foolishly disregarding the economic and social handicaps under which the Outcastes suffer, I said, "You ought to give the sick children milk to drink." Hearing these words the rich man could no longer contain himself. "Yes, you may give them the milk of your own swine," he said, in words the unendurable insult and cruelty of which can only be understood by those who know the attitude taken in the East towards the animal named by the land-owner.

The Outcastes cannot be expected to be anything but filthy in their habits, and sunk in abysmal ignorance and superstition, in view of the scornful hostility and contempt poured out upon them by the rest of the community. I remember about the same time seeing in a village a child who was evidently a sufferer from epilepsy. He bore all over his body the scars of horrible burns which had been inflicted upon him by his parents, probably under the advice of a local outcaste "medicine-man" and in accordance with animistic beliefs, in order to drive out the evil spirit which was supposed to be the cause of his disease. The child's suffering from these burns must have been appalling. They had certainly greatly increased his weakness and the serious nature of the disease from which he was suffering.

The nights were already bitterly cold in that tragic November. In the outcaste quarters of the villages the sick and dying would be lying without any bedding or other means of keeping themselves warm. I recollect urging the one man left as yet untouched by the disease in a largish household, to wrap his wife and sick children up. He replied, "We have no bedding, and nothing else to wrap them in." Then pointing to a bundle of sticks outside the low door of this tiny hut, he said, "That is our bedding." He meant that on the bitter winter nights he and his family would try to keep themselves warm, without possibility of sleep, by cowering over a tiny fire.

There is no exaggerating the pitiableness of the condition of these Outcastes, especially as it is brought home to one when one passes rapidly from village and village, and enters (as is needful at such a time) almost every house. The general impression left upon the mind is that of abysmal and abject poverty, and of hatred and scorn meted out upon the sufferers from the rest of the community through no fault of their own. This impression becomes a burning and passionate desire that something, however revolutionary, may be effected to improve their position.

The condition to which the Outcastes have been reduced is nothing less than a deadly poison eating into the vitals of the body politic in India. It must be remembered that the reason for their degradation is fundamentally the belief that they have been born Outcastes because of wickedness in some previous incarnation on this earth. They are miserable, ignorant, filthy, despised for good reasons, according to this belief. What impertinence and impiety to interfere with the decrees of eternal justice, and attempt to raise them from their degradation! This pernicious line of thought works itself out psychologically as a rationalization of laziness and inertia. The mass of their fellow-countrymen excuse themselves from doing anything about the removal of Untouchability, and defend their own callousness in the matter, by taking refuge in the doctrine of *karma* (reward and punishment for past actions) and re-birth.

All the more honour to Mr. Gandhi that he has taken the problem of the Outcastes seriously: has refused to be deterred by all the rationalizings of corrupt and reactionary orthodoxy: and both by his own example and by the strategy and tactics of his anti-Untouchability campaign has now for twenty-five years been showing India a better way.

But it may well be doubted whether Mr. Ghandi's methods are revolutionary enough. Time passes. It is already nearly a quarter of a century since the pneumonia-time: and there is no very marked change in the position of the Outcastes, at any rate in the villages of the central part of India. In the big cities taboos have been broken, innumerable public buildings and institutions thrown open (largely as a result of the Vaikom incident already described); but what of the villages?

India being what she is, it is probably only by religion that the needful revolution can be brought about. To say this is not to deny the religious basis of Mr. Ghandi's idealism and methods of reform. But they are working too slowly. A religious solution for the problem of their oppression has been found by some Outcastes of the North-west. They have embraced Islam, and thus have stepped out at once into a religious system which is also a social system, and which under both aspects prides itself, not without justice, on its regarding all men as equal in the sight of Allah, and on its implementing in daily social practice this ideal of equality and brotherhood.

But Islam is a fighting religion; and more and more outspokenly the Islamic leaders look to a future in India in which India herself shall have ceased to exist, because the provinces with a Mohammedan majority shall have formed a separate Islamic state, Pakistan—the Holy Land. In effect this will mean certain civil war and the attempt of the Moslems, if they are given a free hand, to re-establish the old Islamic dominion over the whole of India.

Especially in the South another religious solution to the problem of the Outcastes is being discovered. In increasing numbers they are becoming Christians. In many areas this tendency has already become a mass-movement. In spite of the evil example set to the East by the war-making powers of the West, still many of them nominally Christian, Christianity in India is pacifist, in the sense at least that it has no ambitions after making Indian Christians the conquerors of all India. It is also increasingly Indian in its sympathies and aspirations. It sees that Christ has been disastrously misinterpreted by the West; and it believes that as the intense spirituality of the Indian mind is brought to the service of Christ, He will be expressed to the world again in Oriental terms, which will be far nearer the truth than the travesty which the materialistic and warring West has made of Him and His faith. Ideally, not less than Islam, Christianity is a religion of radical equality and uncompromising brotherhood. It is of course easy to point the finger of scorn at the denial of Christ in these respects in the West to-day; but Indian Christianity is becoming increasingly aware of the possibility, and the necessity, of piercing through this Western veneer to the true Eastern Christ in whom all men are effectually brothers.

Thus the coming of the Outcastes into the Christian fold, in ever larger and larger numbers, is not a threat politically to the well-being of India, as in the case of their embracing Islam, nor is it a breaking of allegiance towards their own Oriental heritage. They enter a religion of ideally complete equality and full brotherhood, and a religion which, originating in the East, is instinctively in sympathy with the deepest and best in the Eastern outlook, as shown for instance in Mr. Ghandi.

Christianity has already, in almost innumerable instances, shown that it can exert a revolutionary influence in giving freedom and fullness of life to the Outcastes.

Only to-day I have been told the story of an Outcaste in Eastern Bengal, whose mother became a widow and in complete destitution applied for help to the Christians. Eventually she and her small son became Christians themselves. If the change had not taken place, the boy would (if he survived) have been brought up in the ignorance and extreme poverty which have been described above. As it was, he went first to a village school, and then to College. He became a distinguished scholar and teacher, and spent his life not only in training others for Christian service in India, but also in literary work, for the interpretation of Christ to India. He has recently died, but his son is now secretary and organizer of a large section of the free indigenous Church in Eastern India.

In the past, but now no longer, the British appreciated the great qualities hidden in the Outcastes sufficiently to recruit many Outcaste regiments in the British-Indian army. The traditions of this past still exist, and may be revived. But instances such as that just given show that the actual joining of the Christian Church may effect a revolutionary change in the circumstances of the Outcastes such as no governmental measure can possibly effect. I have myself been personally in contact with many similar cases—Outcaste families, which especially in the second or third generations have reached positions of influence and leadership. There is in the members of such families a certain robustness of outlook and strength of character (probably due, by reaction, to their release from the old situation of oppression, degradation and fear), which means that they are a peculiarly valuable element for good in the re-making of India.

Centuries ago there lived in Western India an Outcaste named Chokamela, who became a devotee of Vishnu, and was rewarded by a vision of the deity whom he adored. By that vision he believed that Vishnu had revealed to him that though untouchable to man he was not untouchable to God but on the contrary very precious. One of the most significant of the reform-movements within modern Hinduism, the Rama-krishna Mission, has set up "Chokamela" Hostels in various educational centres, and is endeavouring to secure (against formidable difficulties) that larger and larger numbers of young Outcastes shall obtain a modern education. This is work of first-class value; and is one more sign of the stirring of the Hindu conscience with regard to this great wrong. There are also many schools for Outcastes run by the Christian Missions. The welfare organization of the large cotton mills at Nagpur in the Central Provinces has organized a model village for mill-hands, the great majority of those living in it being Outcastes. During the political troubles about the year 1920 Outcastes were in some places elected in derision by their Hindu neighbours to the provincial Councils. But in the Councils they learnt their power, and learnt too how to use it. In a typical city the Outcastes number 25,000 out of a total population of 150,000, and constitute by far the largest single bloc of voters.

In these and many other ways, times are changing; and the future of the Outcastes becomes more and more bright, especially as Mr. Ghandi's anti-Untouchability movement gains in influence and momentum.

X

FAMINE

UP TO THE BEGINNING of the present century, in India (as also in Russia, and for similar reasons) widespread and horrible famines, destroying tens of millions of lives, occurred every few years. The most obvious cause was the failure of the rainfall, with the loss of crops, the dying of cattle, and the consequent soaring of food-prices and mass-unemployment of the agricultural population. There being no unemployment benefit and no poor relief in India, the result could only be innumerable deaths.

This primary cause of famine was aggravated by the export of grain,* and the inadequacy of transport-facilities.

After the great famine of 1900, which had followed close on another very serious one in 1897, the Government of India set itself to devise an effective strategy against the recurrence of such appalling calamities. There is always an abundant crop somewhere or other in India, because different parts of the country enjoy such widely differing climates, and depend for their rains upon different monsoon-currents. Therefore, obviously, one main remedy for famine was the steady improvement of the railways, and the extension of them till no part of India should be too far from a railway centre, which could be used in case of need for the organization of emergency food-importation. In consequence, India now stands second only to the United States in the length of her railways.

* £10 million-worth of grain was exported in the disastrous famine-year of 1897.

A second obvious necessity was to get news of the probability of famine-conditions early enough to allow of food-supplies being purchased by government action, and imported in sufficient quantities to provide relief for those who might otherwise starve.

Then there was the problem of agricultural unemployment, and the consequent inability of the people to purchase the supplies which would be brought in. The obvious remedy against this was the starting of public works on a sufficient scale to give employment at an adequate rate of pay, to all the able-bodied unemployed. In the more backward districts, where famine was most probable because of the lack of stored food-supplies, the most necessary form of public works was the construction of roads, irrigation schemes, and wells. The schemes would be chosen largely for the number of people which they gave promise of employing. It would be necessary to construct more or less permanent camps for the workers, who would probably come in from villages scattered over a wide area. In addition, it would be needful to make provision for the weak and the aged, in their own villages, because they would not be able to travel to the relief camps, or to do the hard physical work there provided.

In 1921 I was fortunate enough to be a Famine Charge Officer superintending a section of the working of this Famine Code, as the whole plan is called, in a remote corner of the Central Provinces. The Mandla District is chiefly inhabited by aboriginal tribes. It is extremely hilly, and the hills are covered with forest. There is only one short stretch of narrow-gauge railway, at the opposite side of the District from the part where the famine was worst; and the roads were few and far between and of very inferior quality. It was as severe a test as could be found for the working of the Famine Code.

The District is about the size of Yorkshire, and contains

300,000 inhabitants, living in scattered villages, often separated from each other by twelve or fifteen miles of jungle. There were many man-eating tigers at work in the area; and the people were so terrified of them that economic and agricultural life had largely come to a standstill. "Agricultural life" is indeed largely a misnomer; for many of the aborigines were still practising the primitive shifting cultivation, burning off a fresh patch of jungle each year, and sowing a meagre crop amid the wood-ash in a hastily scratched patch of ground. Their cattle were the real wealth of most of these forest villages; and they had suffered terribly, both from the drought and the consequent lack of grass and water, and from the tigers.

In the North-east of the district where I was working, the Government had long before begun to bring in grain over a mountain range from a single-track railway outside the Mandla District altogether. There was only one road, of an extremely primitive character, and there were supposed to be only twelve wheeled carts available in that area. Consequently the transport was mostly by means of immense herds of pack-animals, chiefly bullocks, but also ponies. In other parts of India herds of sheep and goats are used for the same purpose, each animal carrying a couple of panniers filled with grain. A sufficiency of food for present needs was being steadily brought over the mountains in this way from the nearest railway stations, to which it had been conveyed from places a thousand miles away, where it was plentiful, and had been purchased by Government agency for famine-relief purposes.

Public works had been started, and camps for the workers set up, at a number of places. The people had begun to appreciate the fact that they could earn good money at these camps, and that there was food to be purchased for the money in the store-houses which had been established in connection with the camps, and which were supplied by the pack-trains moving across the mountains from the railway.

The organization, so far as I could see, was working like clockwork, and given a certain amount of intelligent supervision should be almost fool-proof. Later, an appalling cholera epidemic was to upset all our calculations, and to drive the people back in terror from the public works and the relief camps to their distant villages, there to starve or to die of the cholera they had brought with them. But the cholera epidemic was not the fault of the Famine Code or of its administration (except in so far as more adequate provisions might have been made for medical supplies and the presence of doctors); so far as the provision of relief and of food went, the Code worked admirably.

My own special task was in the main the supervision of gratuitous relief in the scattered villages, amongst people too feeble to migrate to the relief camps. I well remember the first village I visited in this way. It stood on the top of a hill. As I approached it, a tall man, terribly emaciated, emerged from a hut, and tottered down the hill towards me. He was coming apparently to tell me about the condition of the people surviving in the village. Before he could reach me, he fell to the ground, and by the time I came up to him he was dead. That was my introduction to the facts of famine. It was an extremely arduous undertaking visiting the scattered jungle villages. The mountain paths were so bad that the only means of reaching distant villages was to walk to them. The weather was extremely hot; and behind every bush in the unending stretches of jungle through which one passed there might have been lurking a man-eating tiger. At each village one was greeted by a pathetic group of the aged, the infirm, the blind, the lame, lepers, people suffering from virulent small-pox and from many other diseases. Each case had to be examined, and the decision made whether gratuitous relief should be given, or whether an attempt should be made to get the patient to hospital, very many miles away. In a few cases the applicant had to be told that he was perfectly fit to go to work on the relief camps. Gratuitous relief is of course a profoundly unsatisfactory form of famine-relief. Payments could only be made in cash, and this left the recipient the necessity of getting the food from the Government store-houses long distances away. Also it has been abundantly proved in India, as in every other country where the plan has been tried, that the actual giving away of cash or commodities pauperizes, destroys self-respect, undermines character, and may in this way do more harm even than famine. Therefore it was necessary to make sure in every case that it was really impossible for the applicant to earn for himself on the relief-works.

With regard to these latter, they were a scene of amazing activity. If a road was being built, there would be gangs of men quarrying stone, gangs of women breaking the stone that had been quarried, for road-metal, gangs of young people carrying the metal in baskets to the site of the new road, where other gangs of men would be digging out the track, or blasting it if necessary, whilst women carried baskets of earth on their heads to form embankments.

During the hot weather the people needed little in the way of living accommodation except rough huts made of branches of trees, which they erected for themselves. They were paid daily, on a piece-work basis; and food-supplies were ready at hand for them to purchase.

I did not understand the matter at the time, but this whole enterprise was a practical illustration of the way in which a Government ought to treat its unemployed. As the famine-conditions intensified and ordinary forms of employment became impossible, public works were opened on a large enough scale to provide employment for everyone needing it, payment being made for work done at rates adequate to maintain health and strength. Later, as unemployment decreased, and normal conditions began to return, the public works in question were reduced accordingly.

In 1931, during his visit to England in connection with the Round Table Conference, I had the privilege of a long talk with Mr. Ghandi on the subject of unemployment in England and Wales. He emphasized that the phenomenon, which at that time was growing to terrifying proportions, must be taken seriously. He declared also that the dole is an insult to human nature: and that the unemployed must be taught to regard it as such, to refuse to accept it, and to "come out on the streets with their wives and families and starve in public rather than accept it" (advice which I have not had the courage to hand on to my unemployed friends). He believed that if they should have the courage and determination to act in this way, the Government would be convinced of the inadequacy and inhumanity of the dole policy, and would be quickly converted to the necessity of doing justice to the unemployed; in other words, they would institute adequate schemes of public works to give employment to all needing it, and they would pay them for their services on these public works at adequate rates.

The fact should never be forgotten that Sweden, which was exceedingly hard hit by the industrial depression of the early nineteen-thirties, did as Mr. Ghandi advised. She organized great schemes for the building of roads, bridges, railways, public buildings, etc. She drafted her workers into such schemes as they came out of ordinary industry; and she paid them at adequate rates for their work. It was an expensive policy, but she paid for it by loans which were designed to be paid off during the prosperous years of the ten-year economic cycle. As a consequence of this courageous and far-sighted policy she kept her workers, who would otherwise have been unemployed, fit and happy, both physically and psychologically. She immensely improved her cities and her countryside. She made Stockholm into an almost unbelievably beautiful and gracious city. She built many admirable Cooperative factories and other public service institutions. She came out of the depression period with her manhood—her most precious possession—unimpaired; and she returned her workers to their ordinary vocations in a country enheartened and inspired by what they had done during the hard years to make her better worth living in. If we had followed Mr. Gandhi's advice, our own country might have trodden the same path. Had we done so, Germany would probably have followed our example. In this case there would have been no mass-unemployment to which Hitler could promise work, and so come into power. There would have been no need for him to keep that promise by re-arming; and therefore there would have been no war.

Though it may have been responsible for many muddles and mistakes in other spheres, the British Government in India, by elaborating and perfecting the Famine Code, and by putting it into practice in 1921 and on other occasions, showed plainly that it has learned how to do the right thing by the unemployed. Mr. Gandhi came from India, where for many years such a policy had been taken for granted as the only right thing to do with mass-unemployment (i.e., famine), and told us in the West, during the worst period of our own distress, that we ought to do as India had done. We paid no heed, and have got the war in consequence.

Ex oriente lux—in regard to this peculiarly Western problem (as we are wont to regard it), mass-unemployment. But we chose the darkness rather than the light.

The onus of keeping the Famine Code in right operation, all over the difficult Mandla District, lay upon the shoulders of a young District Officer. It was a tremendous responsibility.

Once our paths crossed, and I shared his dinner and his tent. The talk was famine, famine, famine: and even after we had got to sleep, he awakened me again and again by muttering in his sleep about the famine. He, and the Code which he was administering, and which (bulky as it is) he knew by heart from cover to cover, represent the British system at its very best. He was constantly amongst the people, in and out of their villages, and hearing from their own lips how everything was going. He spoke their language well, was genuinely interested in them, laughed and joked with them, and was working himself to death to save them. Behind him lay the resources of a great empire, and in the pages of the Famine Code the condensed wisdom, public-spirit and experience of men of good-will in the past.

But why could not we in the West learn from India in time?

NOTE.—As these pages go to the Press, news is coming in of a sudden rise of food-prices in many parts of India. Rice, for instance, is being sold in the Bombay Presidency for the equivalent of a shilling a pound, instead of a penny, and potatoes for 9d., instead of, perhaps, a halfpenny. The process began with the cutting off of the Burma rice supply in 1942. The land-owner and money-lender class (the two are usually one) is also the grain-dealing and grain-storing class. When food-prices begin to rise, they are tempted to hold on, i.e., to hoard, in order to sell at a high profit later. Thus a vicious circle comes into being. Hoarding leads to higher prices and so, through the profit-motive, to more hoarding. It is now (February, 1943) actually announced that we are to ship grain to India, even in the present situation of shipping-shortage. It would take 1,500 ships constantly at work to give the Indian population one slice of bread a day or the equivalent in rice. Yet we established this land-owning, money-lending, grain-dealing class in power, originally by the Permanent Settlement of 1793, and all that has sprung from it. And we depend upon the support of that class for our imperial position in India.

XI

THE CONGRESS

THE INDIAN NATIONAL CONGRESS, which has become the focus-point of national feelings and national aspirations, was launched in 1885 largely under the leadership of two Westerners, Sir William Wedderburn and Mr. A. O. Hume. At the first meeting there were seventy delegates present, who had had to be "pressed and entreated to come." The tone of the discussions was eminently mild, one of the speakers, later a bitter opponent of the British, declaring that "By a merciful dispensation of Providence, India, which was for centuries the victim of external aggression and plunder, of internal civil wars and general confusion, has been brought under the dominion of the great British Power."

At one of the early Congress meetings, as Mr. Gandhi told me in 1931, he was present as a door-keeper, and heard the Congress President quote the words of Cardinal Newman's great hymn, *Lead, Kindly Light:*—

> O'er moor and fen, o'er crag and torrent, till
>   The night is gone.

Ever since, he told me, he has thought of this hymn as applying to his own life.

The Congress continued as an inconspicuous gathering of gentle-spirited Liberals and Moderates, gradually becoming less submissive, till Lord Curzon's impolitic partition of Bengal, early in the present century, stirred up a hornets' nest.

About the same time the victory of Japan over Russia gave an immense impetus to Indian nationalist aspirations, because it was thereby shown that Western nations, for all their wealth and prestige, are not invulnerable, and can even be beaten at their own game of scientific warfare by Orientals. Thus there grew up a spirit of extremism, of which the most notable leader was Mr. B. G. Tilak, a Maratha from Western India. He founded his movement, which was anything but pacifist and came very near to condoning political murder, on the teachings of the *Gita* and on a revival of Hindu religious cults characteristic of the Maratha country.

Meanwhile a new kind of leader was rising to greatness, Mr. G. K. Gokhale. He was the finest orator in the English language that I personally have ever listened to. He was strictly constitutionalist in his attitude, and in this was strenuously opposed to the physical-force extremism of Tilak. He used the opportunities already opening out to Indians in provincial councils and in the central legislature and executive to press for orderly and constructive reform in a great number of directions, especially in connection with questions of finance, of land-tenure and (later) of the position of Indians overseas. He was a really great statesman; and through his friendship with Lord Morley had much to do with the development of democratic institutions in India. His untimely death early in 1915—he really gave his life for India through arduous overwork—was a very great calamity.

In 1916 came the memorable meeting of the Congress at Lucknow, which resulted in a pact between Hindus and Musalmans. By the terms of this agreement separate electorates were to be given to the Musalmans,* and they were to be granted a representation in provincial and central coun-

* This ill-starred concession had already been made in the Minto-Morley Reforms of 1909, which gave a slightly more democratic complexion than before to the provincial Legislatures.

cils slightly higher than that to which their numbers entitled them.

In 1917 a declaration of the British Government promised India self-government by stages after the war then in progress. But in 1919 came the unwisely repressive Rowlatt Acts, and a wave of bitter resentment passed over India; for she had been expecting very different treatment as the result of the services which she had rendered in the war. The movement of protest led by Mr. Gandhi developed, on the unfounded rumour of his arrest, into what the Government regarded as incipient rebellion in the Punjab; and the Amritsar shooting took place. An undetermined number of Indians, perhaps seven hundred or more, were killed and wounded. They were members of an unarmed crowd which had gathered for a prohibited meeting. For years the whole political situation was clouded by the repercussions of this piece of frightfulness; and in consequence the Montagu-Chelmsford reformed constitution of 1919, which came into force a year or two later under fire from Mr. Gandhi's non-cooperation movement, started work under very difficult conditions.

The new constitution divided the administration of the Indian provinces into two parts, the "reserved" departments, administered by the Governor in Council, and the "transferred" departments, which were placed under the care of Indian ministers, chosen by the Governor and working closely with him (in a kind of embryo Cabinet) but responsible to the Provincial Legislature.* It was an awkward and very vulnerable system, obviously only useful for a limited time and as a method of transition to full responsible government. Congress, under Mr. Gandhi's leadership, would at first have nothing to do with it, or with the various steps

* The chief "reserved" subjects were law and order and land-revenue; education, agriculture, public health, forests, cooperation, industrial development, public works were "transferred."

(especially the Simon Commission of 1927 and succeeding years) undertaken in order to prepare the way for the move forward from the existing "Dyarchy" to a more satisfactory democratic system.

The non-cooperation movement of 1920–22 developed into a campaign of "civil disobedience" (non-payment of taxes). There were disturbances, and jailings. Later, in 1930 and the following years, Congress began to plan, still under Mr. Gandhi's leadership, for the deliberate breaking of the law, on a nation-wide scale, in cases where no moral obliquity was involved in such law-breaking. For instance, the salt-monopoly held by Government was deliberately infringed. Traffic regulations were persistently defied, sometimes by crowds numbering several hundred thousand people, and bearing the Congress flag. The Government armed its police with brass-shod *lathis* (clubs), and a great deal of Indian blood was shed, though the discipline imposed by Mr. Gandhi in regard to non-violence was so strictly obeyed by his followers that no English lives were lost. The Congress was declared outlaw; and its leading men, with tens of thousands of their followers, were jailed. During an interval of truce, in 1931, Mr. Gandhi came to England as a member of the Round Table Conference; but renewed conflict broke out soon after his return to India, and there followed several years of police-beatings of unarmed crowds, wholesale jailings and other forms of repression.

Meanwhile, the situation as between Hindus and Musalmans was becoming more and more grave. Unfortunately the Montagu-Chelmsford Reforms, which came into operation in 1921, had adopted the precedent of the Minto-Morley Reforms (1909), and the proposal of the 1916 Lucknow Congress, in regard to communal electorates, with the result that the working of democratic institutions was accompanied by a widening of the rift between the two great communities. We have already noticed that communal electorates mean that only fanatically Hindu Hindus or Moslem Moslems have a chance of election; and that they can only get elected by beating the communal big drum and fomenting and exploiting communal differences. Mr. Gandhi's fast of 1924, undertaken at a time when these differences had developed into civil war, showed that there is a method by which the evil-will of murderous hostility can be turned into the good-will of friendship; but the lesson had been neglected, and is indeed still being neglected; for the pernicious system of separate electorates has not even yet been changed into the beneficent system of joint electorates (in large multi-member constituencies) with reservation of seats for the various committees in accordance with their population. Under this latter system, as we have also noticed, it is only moderate men of both communities who have a chance of being elected, since they have to attract the votes of the other communities as well as of their own. Hitherto the Musalmans have for the most part been implacably opposed to such joint electorates, under which they say they would not feel safe. But the experience of the past twenty years has shown conclusively that to yield to them on this point leads straight to civil war, in which their minority-position renders them liable to extreme sufferings.*

During the whole period since the beginning of the present century, certain parts of India, especially the East, have been subject to oubreaks of revolutionary crime, which takes two main forms, first the murder of Government officials, and second the committing of armed robbery with the object of securing funds for political purposes. From time to time the problem presented by this type of extremism has become so serious that the ordinary law has been set aside by the admin-

* It was only by means of another of Mr. Gandhi's fasts, in 1932, that India was saved from communal electorates for the depressed classes as well as the Moslems!

istration, and energetic (not to say oppressive) methods of restoring peace have been employed. This has particularly been the case in Bengal, where suspected terrorists have been placed for long periods under preventive arrest in a kind of concentration camp. Such conditions have led to an infinitude of resentment and hostility, in the voicing of which the Congress has taken the lead. The growth of Communism has also led to similar repressive measures undertaken by a timid administration feeling itself none too securely seated in the saddle. Here, too, protests have found in Congress their natural organ of expression.

In consequence of these manifold developments, Congress has become by far the most important political factor in British India. For a course of many years it has defied the imperial Government; many thousands of its members, including its most distinguished leaders, have suffered for their convictions in jail, by heavy fines, by beatings from the police or in other ways. Very many of them have died for Congress and its principles. It stands forth as the one force which can effectually resist the imperial Government, and which can bring it about that protests against administrative high-handedness are not merely so much wasted breath.

When the period of Dyarchy came to an end, in 1936, and a new "federal" constitution was brought into application in the British Indian provinces, in eight of those provinces (out of eleven) the elections demonstrated that Congress had an unquestionable right to form the new provincial governments. With some misgivings, Congress accepted the situation, and decided to work the new constitution in the provinces, where full self-government was to be in operation, whilst agitating unwearyingly for the same principle to be applied in the central government, where the Viceroy retained considerable autocratic powers. It is to be noticed that, fortunately for India, it has never yet been possible to introduce at the centre the bastard type of federalism, yoking together the representatives of democratic British Indian provinces with the nominees of despotic Princes, which was proposed in the 1936 constitution.

There followed, in the provinces, what has been called the "honeymoon period," during which Indian ministries were proceeding hot-foot with the task of bringing about, by peaceful and constitutional methods, a profound social revolution (especially as regards money-lending, land-tenure, prohibition, etc.) under the fostering care of a foreign imperialism. Such a phenomenon is unique in history. Great importance attaches to the fact that women took a prominent share in much of the work done. The existence of these Congress governments in the eight provinces was an important factor in enabling Mr. Gandhi to make a beginning, by means of his fast of April, 1939, with the solving of the problem of the Indian State. The sudden resignation of those ministries, as signalizing the gravity of the issues involved, gave the imperial Government the moral backing which it needed from India as a whole in order to enable it to support Mr. Gandhi against the Princes.

This interesting epoch of constructive revolution by Indian hands came to an untimely end in September, 1939, when India was brought into the war by the Viceroy's declaration, without her consent being asked. The result was the resignation of the Congress ministries in the eight provinces, and a return to autocratic rule under the provincial governors. Mr. Gandhi's deep pacifist convictions prevented his having anything to do with the support of the war; and his influence succeeded in keeping the Congress aloof from it. When Russia was attacked, in June, 1941, Jawahirlal Nehru, the second most important Congress leader, became restive at the prevailing pacifist attitude. The Japanese conquest of Burma early in 1942 increased Nehru's personal desires for a pro-war policy in Congress, and for a direct relationship of cooperation between India and Russia. At the same time he is equally with Gandhi insistent on the necessity that India should be given immediate self-government, and should not be fobbed off with post-war promises.

In April, 1942, when the Japanese were already thundering at the eastern portal of India, the British Government made an ill-thought-out attempt through the personal agency of Sir Stafford Cripps, to secure whole-hearted Indian cooperation in the war by provision for a constituent assembly to settle the post-war constitution. The Cripps proposals suffered from three radical defects. In the first place they promised that any province or association of provinces which wished to contract out of the new Indian Union could do so and form a free and independent State. In other words, separate nationhood ("Pakistan") was offered to the Moslem provinces. In the second place the same kind of thing was offered, more indefinitely, to Princes or groups of Princes who might wish to contract out. These two proposals would have led inevitably to the Balkanisation of India and to a period of fierce and protracted civil war. In the third place the Princes were offered a third part of the "representation," through their nominees, in the post-war constituent assembly. This would have ensured the predominance of reactionary and anti-democratic forces in that assembly, and would have rendered the proposed "federalism" a farce.

But it was not for any of these reasons that the Ghandi-followers in Congress rejected the Cripps proposals. It was because those proposals did not offer immediate and full self-government; and (less directly) because they involved the abandonment of Mr. Ghandi's and Hindu India's traditional pacifism.

XII

THE INDIAN STATES

THERE ARE 584 Indian States. Their total area is roughly two-fifths of the whole country. Their size varies from that of a largish national State in Europe to that of a smallish English parish. Their rulers enjoy an extraordinary variety of powers; and the degrees in which sovereignty has been divided between the paramount power and the individual States provide an almost inexhaustible mine of interesting study for the constitutional lawyer.

The great majority of these States came into existence well over a hundred years ago, as the result of temporary situations of crisis developing in the struggles between the East India Company and the French, the rulers of Mysore, the Marathas, the Sikhs or other enemies. For reasons now long forgotten, and in many cases not bearing very close investigation, the ruler of a given State at that distant date allied himself with the Company. As a reward he got a treaty which guaranteed himself and his descendants in the possession of their territory, the understanding being that if enemies within or without attempted to eject him (or his descendants), British bayonets would be supplied in sufficient numbers to enable him to retain his position.

At the time when these treaties were made the States were governed by traditional autocratic methods. Having received such a guarantee, the rulers and their descendants, with certain honourable exceptions, continued and continue still to govern their territories in the same way. As the generations have passed, democratic tendencies have awakened and come to strength in neighbouring British Indian provinces, but the States have slumbered on, still governed (again with a few honourable exceptions) by the old autocratic methods.

Unfortunately for the Princes, however, there is a fundamental natural law which declares that if an organism ceases to struggle, it begins to atrophy, to degenerate, to become parasitic and eventually extinct. The Princes have been artificially segregated from the struggle for existence, and no amount of treaties from a paramount power, however wise and powerful, can protect them from the operation of that law. Hence in many instances the government of the States has steadily become worse. A great many of the rulers fail to distinguish between their private income and the revenue of the State, and spend in personal luxury of many types (some of them lurid) the monies which are wrung from a cruelly impoverished peasantry, and which should be used for their benefit. Many of the rulers inevitably look upon their dominions and the people in them with a proprietor's feelings. Their position is not unlike that of the great Russian land-owners before the emancipation of the serfs in 1861, in the period, that is, when a serf might be exchanged for a hose-pipe or a greyhound. In some ways the Indian ruler is in a stronger position; for there is a much less effective central control exercised by the paramount power over the States than was exercised even by a reactionary Tzar over the great Russian land-owners.

The subjects of the States have no rights against their rulers, except in cases like Mysore, Travancore, Baroda, where constitutions have been introduced. Elsewhere, "if an autocratic ruler confiscates property and imprisons for no reason, there is no court to which appeal can be made and no authority which will uphold just rights." * The only refuge is

* Panikkar "Indian States."

revolution: and then, if revolution breaks out, the British are bound by treaty to march in, and to suppress the rebels.

I remember talking many years ago with a young British military officer who had been called in this way to put down a rebellion in a remote central Indian State. The rebellion had been caused by infamous and prolonged misgovernment on the part of the State ruler. The peasants had left their villages in despair and had taken to the jungle as outlaws. When this occurs in the East, as in mediaeval England, it is certain proof of serious governmental injustice. The English officer had had to shoot down these poor peasants, who were armed with nothing but bows and arrows; and he told me in no uncertain terms what he thought of the job, and of the system under which he was obliged to prostitute his honour in such a fashion.

I have myself lived for many years within a few hundred yards of the border of a large Indian State, and have no hesitation at all in saying from my own personal observations that the present system of things demands radical and immediate change. The States form a vast relic of feudalism; and the paramount power has no business to buttress itself by their support. How can we pretend that we stand for democracy and freedom in the West, when our power rests on such foundations in the East?

For it must be recognized that any imperial power ruling a conquered people which has begun to become conscious of its subject position and of its right to self-governing nationhood, is bound to find allies amongst the people it rules. The only allies available will be reactionary elements which profit by the existing imperial relationship. The Romans adopted this expedient in their government, for instance, of Palestine, allying themselves with the high-priestly families, which were also great land-owners and exploiters of the profitable vested interests connected with the Temple in Jerusalem. In each country of Europe which the Germans conquered in the war of 1939 they found themselves compelled to set up puppet governments recruited from similar reactionary elements in the population. The Japanese have done the same in China. The Indian States form an immense practical demonstration of the same principle. Their loyalty to the imperial Government is unquestionable. They come forward eagerly to offer their States' resources, the property not of themselves but of their subjects, to the paramount power in time of war; but in time of peace they will stand forth in their true light as enclaves of autocratic reaction, to which the paramount power may retreat if things become too hot in British India.

Thus the States are a menace to the future freedom and unity of a democratic and self-governing India.

Twenty years ago, before giving self-government to Eire, we set up an enclave forming an imperial foothold in Ulster. We have realized since then that in so doing we have prevented the chance of reconciliation between ourselves and Eire, and have hence laid upon our own backs an extremely heavy burden in the war of 1939, when the ports of Eire became a vital need to us. In India we are in danger of preparing not one but scores, even hundreds, of Ulsters, with an aggregate population of ninety-three millions, and lying not in one corner of the country only, but on all the main lines of communication and in strategic positions along the frontiers. Many of these States are already armed, and they possess the only military forces in existence in India not under direct British control. It follows that any attempt to give self-government to British India which does not at the same time deal radically with the problem of the States cannot but be a cruel farce. As with Ulster, the imperial forces would merely have to retire within the frontiers of the States, and remain there in readiness to return. Under such circumstances there could be no Indian independence, no Indian settlement of the communal problem, no real Indian responsibility.

Even if, by agreement, the British forces were to withdraw entirely from India, unless the problem of the States were solved, we should only be leaving the country as a whole at the mercy of the State armies. Definite and fearless planning is therefore necessary in regard to the States; and that planning should be implemented at the earliest possible moment.

A leading article in *The Times* spoke thus of the States, in 1853:—

We have emancipated these pale and ineffectual pageants of royalty from the ordinary fate that awaits an oriental despotism . . . It has been well said that we give these Princes power without responsibility. Our hand of iron maintains them on the throne, despite their imbecility, their vices and their crimes. The result is in most of the states a chronic anarchy, under which the revenues of the states are dissipated between the mercenaries of the camp and the minions of the Court. The heavy and arbitrary taxes levied on the miserable peasants serve only to feed the meanest and the most degraded of mankind. The theory seems in fact admitted that the Government is not for the people but the people for the king, and that so long as we secure the king his sinecure royalty, we discharge all the duty that we, as Sovereigns of India, owe to his subjects who are virtually ours.

There is much in this indictment which still stands true. The real fact of the matter is that the States are an anachronism, and a dangerous anachronism. They are going to be a more dangerous anachronism still if they are permitted to endure as they are at present into the post-war period of constitution-making. Both in the so-called federal constitution of 1936, and in the Cripps proposals of 1942, the British Government shows that it conceives it possible, and desirable, to "federate" the despotically-governed States with the democratic provinces of British India, and to give self-government to the total fabric so formed. But it cannot be too strongly insisted that no true federalism can exist as between autocratic princes and democratic provinces. The essence of the federal idea is that the Union is a Union not of governments but of peoples. Representation for the federal assemblies is based, fundamentally and essentially, on direct election by the populations of the uniting territories. The presence of the Princes' nominees in the federal legislature, to the suggested extent of one-third of the total membership, would inevitably corrupt the whole body, and make reaction dominant.

Meanwhile the existence of these despotic rulers as our allies, in what we represent as a democratic cause, seriously weakens the effectiveness of our propaganda and compromises our good faith, especially in American eyes.

Are the States then to be scrapped wholesale, and their territories annexed to the nearest British Indian provinces? Some Indian extremists would recommend as much. But we need not agree with them. In the first place, the Indian States are invaluable as repositories—it is to be feared that they may soon be the sole remaining repositories—of genuine Indian art, music, architecture and culture generally. In the second place, they are invaluable as experiment-stations for genuinely Indian forms of government, law and administration. In the third place, they serve as training-schools for Indian statesmanship and Indian wisdom in many spheres. The high qualities which they may help to develop in this direction may be illustrated by the following distinguished opinion:—

The Lord Chancellor did not give the Native Judges too high a character when he said in the House of Lords in 1883, as the result of his experience of Indian cases appealed to the Privy Council, that in respect of integrity, of learning, of knowledge, of the soundness and satisfactory character of the judgments arrived at, the judgments of the Native Judges were quite as good as those of the English.*

* Strachey, *India*, quoted in Ramsay Macdonald, *The Government of India*.

No doubt the smaller States, or many of them, might without disadvantage be incorporated with neighbouring provinces; but it is obvious that great loss will be incurred, and not by India alone, if some solution for the problem of the States is not found which will enable the more notable among them to survive as separate entities, though with abuses corrected.

To this end the paramount power should insist immediately that constitutions shall be introduced into all States of a certain size and importance, in imitation of those already in force in the few progressive States. At the same time extensive schemes of popular education must be set on foot. The way of advance here also has already been shown by such a State as Baroda. The constitutions must provide for the introduction of democratic institutions as rapidly as possible; and without popular education democracy will be a farce.

By such a process of reform the State rulers will become constitutional sovereigns, who reign but do not rule; and their domains will become fitted to enter the new Indian Federation in the only safe and adequate way, that is, through electing their own representatives to the federal assemblies by popular vote. At the same time what is valuable in the position of the States, as the true Indian India, and in the State-tradition of art, culture, government, administration and statesmanship, will be preserved.

In certain cases, especially those of the smaller States which are incorporated with neighbouring provinces, the rulers should receive compensation, and be pensioned off, as has not infrequently occurred in the past. Everywhere it will be necessary to revise ancient treaties; and this must be done courageously, but at the same time generously; due compensation being given for privileges lost.

In conclusion, it is common for speakers and thinkers in England, in dealing with the situation in India, totally to ignore the problem of the States; but it cannot be too emphatically stated that this problem is of urgent first-class importance to the whole future in that country. Unless it be solved, and solved speedily and radically, but at the same time generously, there can be no hope of peace, unity and freedom.

* NOTE.—A recent British writer, friendly to the States, which he knows well, speaks of them in relation to our imperial power as "a network of friendly fortresses." The position could not be more succinctly put.

XIII

EDUCATION

IT CANNOT BE doubted that one of the gravest indictments against the British system in India is the fact that after so many generations of our rule the vast mass of the people still remains illiterate. Only one Indian in eight knows how to read and write. At the other end of the scale, there is an immense and politically dangerous mass of middle-class unemployment, especially amongst men who have spent many years of their life, at great sacrifice financially, in obtaining University degrees.

These two phenomena, mass-illiteracy amongst the peasants and workers, and mass-unemployment amongst the graduates, are obviously in close connection, and point to the fact that the Indian educational system, as we have organized it, is extremely top-heavy. That system was designed by a foreign imperialist government, with the object of supplying itself with an adequate number of well-trained recruits for subordinate official posts. In other words, we devised Indian education as a means of helping ourselves to govern India. This being so, Indian education was faultily planned from the start. The man mainly responsible was Thomas Babington Macaulay, who with a cheerful ignorance declared in 1836:—

It is my firm belief that if our plans of education are followed up, there will not be a single idolater among the respectable classes in Bengal thirty years hence. And this will be effected without any effort to proselytize; without the smallest interference in the religious liberty; merely by the natural operation of knowledge and reflection.

94

Finding the Indian vernaculars deficient in modern literature of the type he approved, Macaulay proceeded to plan to
educate India out of "idolatry" by means of instruction given
in the English tongue. Incredible as it may seem, this system
still survives in a large number of secondary schools and in a
still larger proportion of colleges. It corresponds to the fact
that English is still in the main the language of the higher
branches of administration. But let anyone in this country who
doubts that the Indian educational system has been wrongly
designed by the British imagine what it would have meant to
himself to receive most of his secondary and all his higher education through the medium of (say) Russian! It is unnecessary
to point out what an immense additional burden of time and
trouble, and nervous strain, would have been laid upon him.
Let him realize also that the young people who receive this
education are almost to a man (and a woman) ardent nationalists, and that they are compelled to receive their education in
the tongue of their country's conquerors and by a plan designed to equip those conquerors with sufficient re-enforce-
ments of trained and disciplined clerks and officials!

Such an imperialistic conception of instruction will obviously not care much about popular and elementary education.
Indeed the attitude will probably be found well represented
amongst the governing race (as is in fact the case) that the less
education among the masses the better, for the more they are
educated the harder they will be to control! This same attitude was to be noticed, by the way, amongst the governing
class in England in the days before education became universal and compulsory.

It is true that for the last twenty years education has been
under the control of Indian ministers in the provinces; but
the complaint has been universal amongst these ministers that
their department has been starved. So large a percentage of
the Indian revenue goes on the maintenance of the army and

of the bureaucracy that the "nation-building" aspects of government, notably education, have been grievously undersupplied. In spite of this fact definite and encouraging progress has been effected by the Indian ministers, even amounting to the introduction of schemes of compulsory education in certain areas.*

Mr. Ghandi is convinced, not only that the Indian educational system, having been set up by a foreign imperialism with its own ends in view, has been misconceived from the beginning, but also that this system is far too literary and academic. He wishes to see a popular education very much more closely related to the actual life and needs of the peasantry, with an emphasis on hand-work, on practical community-service and on the study of nature. He has launched his own system of schools designed from the point of view of these ideals; and in so doing has rendered a practical service to his country of the greatest significance. He believes that the school should be an active agency in the combating of the terrible problem of agricultural unemployment; and he tries to send out his pupils, after their course is finished, not only equipped with a sufficiency of the three R's to enable them to understand the money-lender's accounts and the assessments of the revenue collector, but also with a knowledge of how to earn extra money for themselves and their families during the seasons when no work can be done on the fields. If India is to be free and democratic, popular education must penetrate sufficiently far down amongst the peasantry to give them the power of using a vote wisely, and of discriminating between various conflicting political programmes. There can be no doubt that an all-round practical education of the type which Mr. Ghandi has devised, and which is now running

* India spends 1/6 per annum per head of her population on education, Japan 16/6. Education is the only true method of curbing big population increases.

in a great number of schools inspired by him, is better calcu-
lated to produce a peasantry and a working-class capable of
using their votes well, than the almost wholly literary instruction of the British system. For one thing, bitter experience
shows that the existing elementary education is so far divorced
from the realities of life, especially in rural areas, that the
young people who have been through the schools forget
everything they have learned there in a surprisingly short space
of time!

Elementary education has of course always been in the
vernacular, and considerable advance has been made of recent
years, under the guidance of Indian Ministers of Education,
in the process of the vernacularization of secondary education. The vernaculars have however been neglected and despised for so long, as a result partly of over-emphasis on education in English, that considerable literatures have to be
created almost *de novo* if vernacular secondary education is
to be culturally satisfactory. Much can be done by translation;
but this produces a second-hand and derivative type of culture; and there is always the handicap of the difficulty of
securing publication; for there are so many vernaculars, and
the educated class in each of them, and preferring to buy
books written in the vernacular rather than books written in
English, is still so small, that the financial risks of publication
are often very considerable.

Then again there is a whole range of mountainous difficulties presented by the great number of the vernaculars. In the
city where I lived for a number of years there were ten vernaculars, each of them in everyday use as their mother-tongue
by a considerable section of the inhabitants. I was there when
the change-over began from English to the vernaculars as the
medium of instruction in secondary schools. The problem of
providing instruction in ten languages instead of one was
baffling indeed! There was a deeper difficulty still. Secondary

education in the vernacular, in localities where there are a number of vernaculars in everyday use by largish groups, leads to the development of a language-patriotism which often becomes dangerously divisive. The Hindi-speakers will acclaim their own mother-tongue as the simplest and most widely-spread of all the Indian languages, and will hold a two days "conference" in Hindi, ending up with a public performance of a Hindi drama. The real object of the said "conference" is to boost Hindi language-patriotism and to provide propaganda for the adoption of Hindi as the Indian national language. Thereupon, not to be outdone, the Marathi-speakers acclaim Marathi as the "sweetest" of all Indian languages: and hold a three days' "conference" in Marathi. This stirs up the Bengali-speakers, and so forth.

This language-patriotism is not a trivial matter. One cause of the murderous hostility between Hindus and Moslems is the fact that in many parts of India they speak different languages, the Moslems being very language-patriotic for their Hindustani; and however ridiculous it may appear for Hindi-speakers and Marathi-speakers to hate each other just because they do not understand each other, the fact remains that they are inclined so to hate each other, and that the vernacularization of secondary education increases this tendency. It also increases the tendency to disunion between the various parts of India; for roughly speaking each of the big provinces speaks a language (or languages) of its own.

It is probable that Russia shows us the right line of advance here, as with the problem of Indian education as a whole. Just as the "dark masses" of the Russian peasantry have been educated in a remarkably few years, by a resolute attempt, fostered and financed by the central government, to bring a simple and practical form of education into every village, for adults as well as for children, so the far more numerous "dark masses" of the Indian peasantry may be illuminated, and by similar methods. So also with regard to the problems of language-patriotism. The Russian system is to allow the maximum of vernacularization, and indeed actively to encourage from the centre vernacular culture and art; and at the same time to expedite a process of active devolution which, within the strongly-knit federation of the Soviet Union, will grant the maximum of autonomy to each language-group in its own subsidiary republic. In Indian terms this principle will mean, first a new delimitation of provincial frontiers, in order to make them correspond as closely as possible to language-groupings, second a rigorous decentralization of governmental functions in order to give the maximum of autonomy to each of the newly-delimited provinces. In the big metropolitan centres, where a number of cultures and languages meet, there will still be the educational problem of providing instruction in a variety of vernaculars; but this will be lightened of the dangerous divisive tendencies already referred to, since each language-group will have its own acknowledged home-land to which to look.   50899

Christian Missions have been responsible for much important pioneering work in education. They have developed residential schools for girls, for famine-victims, for members of backward groups, special methods of instruction in connection with the naturalizing of such Western innovations as the "project method" or the "Dalton plan," interesting schemes for the development of character and initiative (for instance through boy scouting and community-service), and a great range of admirable elementary school work. In the early days they were pioneers with the development of secondary and higher education; but under modern conditions it may be doubted whether this is their true form of service. Not only are the high schools and colleges nurseries for government servants. They are also, unfortunately, training-institutions for a rapacious middle-class, subsisting largely by oppressive landownership and by money-lending. In this sense it may not unjustly be said that such institutions exist to "give brains to the Devil," and therefore form a none-too-suitable sphere for missionary enterprise and the expenditure of mission money! In the past it has been claimed that these disadvantages are offset by the fact that Christian instruction has been systematically given as an ordinary item in the school programme; but with non-Christian Indian Ministers in charge of education this is becoming less and less possible, and in view of imperialism, and of the catastrophic fall of Western prestige that has come with the wars of 1914 and 1939, a Christianity propagandized in this way meets with more and more psychological resistance amongst the pupils. The future of Missionary education is therefore probably to be sought more in the realm of experiment and adaptation of Western educational discoveries amongst younger pupils.

The future of Indian education as a whole is obviously bound up with the general advance of India towards self-governing nationhood. It is for Indians themselves, under Indian leadership and with Indian inspiration, to tackle the vast problem of peasant illiteracy, and to transform the educational system from the nursery of a governing class, often rapacious and sold to the foreigner, into a creative movement of national culture. Much has already been done. During the twenty years period in which education has been in the hands of Indian ministers, the number of literates has doubled. There are now seventeen universities, with 120,000 students, and over fifteen million pupils are in schools. Such progress is good, but nothing like good enough!

XIV

THE STUDENTS

INDIAN STUDENTS, about whom I may claim to know something, as I spent fifteen years of close comradeship with them, are extremely sensitive, amazingly attractive and interesting, deeply lovable, and politically as inflammable as the Indian forest in summer!

In common with most of the rest of their countrymen they are far better practical psychologists than we Westerners: and it is a most educative process (to oneself, I mean) to go through a play of Shakespeare, or any poem or essay descriptive of character, with a class of them, and to give them their head at the task of unravelling the various psychological complexities in the characters sketched therein. If the teacher can remain in the background and allow them really to express their opinions, he is amazed at the acuteness of analysis which even quite young and inexperienced pupils can give. *Hamlet,* where the characterization is often so baffling, is a good case in point. Once with a junior class I obtained a memorable series of opinions regarding Tennyson's *Simeon Stylites.*

In personal relationships with these students everything depends upon courtesy and friendship. A great friend of mine, now in a distinguished position in Bengal, was once during his student days travelling by train at night. He got out at a station to get a drink of lemonade: the train started again unexpectedly, and he had to make a dash for the nearest carriage. It happened to be a first-class, with one Englishman in it. The trains in India do not have corridors. The Englishman said, "Get out." The Indian student replied, "The train has already started, please let me stay till the next station." The Englishman said, "Get out." The student said, "I can't: it's going too fast. Please let me stand in the corner here till the next station." The Englishman said, "Get out or I shall kick you out"; and he showed that he meant what he said. My friend had to jump for it. The train was already beyond the platform, and gathering speed fast. He got a bad fall, and minor injuries, and lost his luggage, and so forth. The incident, which probably to the Englishman was a trivial business connected with keeping up white prestige and enforcing railway regulations, branded itself indelibly on the Indian's mind.

When you really get to know Indian students well, you will almost always find somewhere in the background an incident like this. If it did not happen to the person you are talking to, it happened to his father, or uncle, or friend, or to someone from the same home-neighbourhood. The memory of it has rankled and festered; and the extreme anti-British attitude adopted by many students may in innumerable instances be traced back to the resentment engendered by such occurrences.

The Mutiny of 1857 is now the better part of a century back; but the mind of India as a whole has not forgotten the atrocities which accompanied its suppression, when the English "chuckled to hear how General Neill had forced high Brahmins to clean up the blood of the Europeans murdered at Cawnpore, and then strung them up in a row, without giving them the time requisite for the rites of purification": and when "Neill's executions were so numerous and so indiscriminate, that one of the officers attached to his column had to remonstrate with him on the ground that if he depopulated the country he could get no supplies for the men": or when an enquiry into the murder of two Indian drivers by newly-arrived British soldiers led to the following explanation, "I seed two Moors (Indians) talking in a cart. Presently I heard one of 'em say 'Cawnpore.' I knowed what that meant; so I fetched Tom Walker, and he heard 'em say 'Cawnpore,' and he knowed what that meant. So we polished 'em both off."

The evil legacy of this distant frightfulness endures, and is reinforced by more recent memories, for example, of the fact that down to quite recent times the murder of Indians by Englishmen was by no means an infrequent occurrence, but rarely met with adequate punishment.*

The students are sensitive in their attitude towards Europeans because they know these facts, and have brooded upon them, and realize that so long as British imperialism endures in India this kind of thing will be apt to recur. Therefore the European who desires to make friends with them, and to enable them to express the best that is in them, has a long handicap against him and a lot of leeway to make up.

At any time of political unrest (and in a country under foreign domination such times come frequently) the Indian students catch the excitement soonest, keep it longest, and are more deeply affected by it than other classes in the community. They are great hero-worshippers, and very susceptible and easily led. I remember well the immense impression produced on a student audience in Delhi in 1913 by the Right Hon. G. K. Gokhale's description, in a most impressive speech, of the sufferings of Indians in South Africa. There was a heartfelt readiness after that meeting amongst the students to do anything and go anywhere that Gokhale might desire, in order to help the sufferers.

Years later, on the death of Mr. B. G. Tilak, the physical-force revolutionary of Western India, there was a most re-

* The quotations reproduced above, from the Russell *Diary* and G. O. Trevelyan's *Competition Wallah*, are given in G. T. Garratt's *An Indian Commentary*: in which other instances may be found (e.g., of the wiping-out of all the men inhabiting certain villages).

markable exhibition of spontaneous grief amongst the students in the Central Provinces, who came to college classes in the garb of Hindu mourning. Well before that time Mr. Gandhi had begun to exercise an extraordinary dominance over their minds. During the Christmas vacation of 1920 he had laid before Congress his policy of non-cooperation, which had been accepted. One item of this policy declared that students should leave all schools and colleges maintained by Government or receiving grants from Government. At the end of the autumn term the college in which I was then serving had well over three hundred pupils. When it re-opened after the Christmas vacation, the numbers had been reduced to about twenty. It took years of patient work before we could get back to our former position. The students who left were sacrificing both past and future. Their parents had out of their poverty laboriously collected the monies needful for seeing them through secondary school and for maintaining them during the time they had spent in college. Their one hope of obtaining a good position in life was to continue their college studies till they obtained degrees. Yet all this they gave up gladly at the call of their country, uttered to them by Mr. Gandhi.

In a typical instance one of these students, a Musalman, intelligent, hard-working and popular even with his Hindu fellow-students, after giving up his studies went to spend the rest of his life as teacher in a national school (one of the new kind organized by Mr. Gandhi without any dependence on Government) in a remote village.

Later on, as Mr. Gandhi grew older, the students' admiration was gradually transferred to Jawahirlal Nehru, who became more and more popular with them on account of his fearless outspokenness and his frequent sufferings in jail. But whoever the leader might be who was the object of their hero-worship for the time being, the students gave him their enthusiastic and whole-hearted allegiance. Nothing could be done by criticizing their favourite; for their hero-worship lay in a sphere of emotion much deeper than logic. All that one could do, if one wanted to help them, was to keep off political discussions, and wait till a change of favour began to manifest itself.

Practically without exception the students are trenchantly, even bitterly, critical of Western civilization as a whole. They are acquainted at first hand with the horrors caused by it in the slums around the mills in any great industrial city of India. They know that these horrors are rooted in love of money and zeal for personal profit and advantage. They know also that these motives lead ultimately to war, and that Western civilization is therefore doomed to end in self-destruction by scientific murder on a colossal scale. These ideas do not come to them, except in a small minority of cases, from Communist propaganda. They come to them as Indians, from their acquaintance with the Indian world-outlook which has been traditional for three thousand years, and which finds its fullest expression in that amazingly complex document, the *Gita*.

The students desire passionately to save their country from the menace of this Western world-view. They see from the obvious instance of Japan the damage done to an Eastern nation which prostitutes its true heritage by wholesale and undiscriminating imitation of the West. They admire Gandhi because he has seen the issues involved clearly, and has set up once more the ancient Indian ideal of a self-denying and rigorously pacifist community-service (the performing of "dharma"—one's personal function in life—for the sake of God and other men, not of oneself). They admire Nehru because he also has clearly perceived the issues involved, and is endeavouring to set up the ideal of a collectivist commonwealth.

Thus the patriotism of the Indian student is very different

from the shallow-pated jingoistic nationalism which too often passes for patriotism amongst students in the West. The Indian is profoundly conscious of being heir to a great spiritual heritage. He sees clearly whither Western industrialism, Western nationalism, Western imperialism are bound. He is desperately anxious that his country should be saved in time from treading the same path, the primrose path to the everlasting bonfire down which Japan is racing so merrily. And he sees the true way of national salvation, in a new collectivism based on the individual citizen's doing his duty to God, man and India for that duty's sake, and not for pay or dividends.

Japan is an ever-present portent to the Indian student. Here is a great Oriental nation, only a generation ago the object of fervent admiration on account of her defeat of Russia, but now disastrously corrupted and demoralized by slavish Westernization. First came industrialization: then as home markets were saturated with the products of the new Japanese factories, there was a hunt for foreign markets by peaceful means, including government subsidies on a vast scale: lastly, as over-production did its work in bringing on acute industrial depression in the home-land, 'the Japanese were driven by imperious necessity to try to seize foreign territories by force, in order to obtain both sources of raw materials and readily-exploitable markets. Once this process of international brigandage was begun, it went forward by leaps and bounds till it became a rapacious imperialism threatening the whole East.

These things the Indian student sees, grimly set forth in a nation whose armies are now thundering at the eastern gateway of his own country. He desires therefore to save India from imperialism, not only from the reigning British imperialism, not only from the attacking Japanese imperialism, but from imperialism as a whole, from the evil spirit which has its roots in industrial individualism and affects like leprosy the whole life of the nations that yield to it, making them outlaws, robbers and murderers.

The Westerner who would really understand the Indian student has to live in very close contact with him, sharing his games, his leisure-pursuits, his home-life (if he is lucky enough to receive an invitation), as well as his studies. From time to time it should be possible to arrange holiday excursions with parties of students, perhaps a walking-tour in the Himalayas, or adventurous explorations in the forests and amongst the mountains of the central part of India. I have had a share in many such expeditions, and look back to them with the greatest possible satisfaction, not merely because of the wonderful country discovered, but because on such shared holidays it is possible more perhaps than in any other way to get behind the students' sensitiveness and reserve, and to understand what they really feel and think, and what they are worth as comrades and friends.

My mind goes back to an occasion many years ago when on one such excursion a large party of us were benighted in the forest, amongst very precipitous mountains, and at last found refuge in a hermit's cave. Rather to our relief the holy man was away, but we made a fire, dried our clothes, which had been soaked by torrential rain, shared such food as we possessed (caste did not seem to matter here), and talked far into the night, till one by one, tired out, we went to sleep, with very insufficient couches of leaves between ourselves and the rock floor of the cave. It is not in the class-room, or the lecture-hall, but on occasions like this that one really gets to know Indian students.

Then there are other occasions, when a sudden dreadful necessity for relief, in time of famine, flood or epidemic, calls out the students to do what they can, in very practical ways, for the country they love so much. If this relationship of friendship has been formed aright, there will be no more loyal and self-sacrificing comrades than these Indian students. At such times barriers of race and creed completely melt away.

A word must be said in conclusion regarding Indian students in this country. They are often exceedingly lonely, and unfortunately have to put up with many slights and rudenesses. They also tend to react violently against the Western life in which they find themselves steeped. They are however peculiarly open to the influence of a genuinely disinterested friendship; and invaluable work may be done for reconciliation between East and West by offering them such friendship, especially in the form of generous hospitality. A large proportion of these men are destined eventually to occupy positions of dignity and leadership in India. They need friendship bitterly whilst they are in England; and the giving of such friendship may exercise a deep influence on them and their country in the future.

XV

HINDUISM

THERE IS A striking lack of comprehension in most definitions of Hinduism. To some who attempt such definitions Hinduism is (and rightly) a majestic system of philosophy, leading the soul forward into the shining mysteries of deeply spiritual religion. To others, it is (and rightly) a vast organization of ceremonial observance, laying its claim upon a man from long before his birth till long after his death. To yet others, it is (and rightly) a fascinating field of study concerning the survival value of primitive animistic superstitions and their capacity for transformation into esoteric cultus. To others again, it is (and rightly) a system of thought and behaviour built up round the central conception of the Transmigration of Souls, and therefore gravely affected by pessimism, social supineness, and world-rejection.

We have already mentioned the three great pathways which Hinduism offers to the soul seeking to become released from the necessity of returning over and over again to this mortal sphere with all its suffering—the Pathway of Deeds, the Pathway of Knowledge, and the Pathway of Devotion. We may find them all three set forth in the *Gita*, by far the most important single document for those studying Hinduism. Here the Pathway of Deeds is represented by the teaching that men must perform their caste-function faithfully, without seeking for personal reward, as an act of service to God and to the community. The Pathway of Knowledge is represented by the deep philosophical teaching of the unity of the individual soul with the Absolute Reality. Above all the Way of Devotion is represented, in the teaching that Release is to be won through personal love for and trust in the incarnation of the Absolute Reality in Krishna, the charioteer of the soul. This great document is in intention an eirenicon between the followers of the Three Pathways; but no one can read it without realizing why it has in effect become the main authority for the followers of the Pathway of Devotion. Its unknown writer was clearly a broad-minded and tolerant teacher who recognized to the full what was true and noble in the two more ancient Pathways, but who held at the same time—and rather as a matter of personal experience than as a matter of logic—that the Pathway of Devotion was the one for himself and for the great mass of his hearers and readers.

Later there came, in the profundities of the teachings of Shankara, a revival of Hindu philosophy, and a return to the Pathway of Knowledge. Release from rebirth is to be found as the soul, all earthly allegiances laid aside, comes in the depth of its secret and individual being to the knowledge that "Thou art That," i.e., that it is itself one with the Absolute Reality. Only so, in the vivid focal-point of this knowledge, can the past be laid aside, with all it holds of necessity for reward and punishment in future rebirths, and the final blessedness of non-return be won.

Centuries later again, with Ramanuja and Ramananda, came another revival of the teaching of release by Devotion; and a little later again the intensely interesting attempt of Kabir to reach a middle way between Hinduism and Islam—an attempt which led to the creation of some of the very finest of all Indian religious poetry. But such syncretism was not destined to prevail; and in the centuries between Kabir and our own time Islam became more intolerant of Hindu "idolatry," while Hinduism developed a great mass of ardent witnessings regarding the certainty of Release through Devotion offered to this or that manifestation of the Ultimate Truth. In the eighteenth century, which was a century of stagnation and retrogression in India as in the West, debased popular cults and rites began to appear or re-appear extensively, notably the insistence on the burning of widows when their husbands died, and the practice of self-immolation by fanatical ascetics beneath the wheels of the huge car of Jagganath, together with hook-swinging, religious murder, infanticide, and similar monstrosities.

With the impact of Western thought and belief, early in the nineteenth century, a wide-reaching transformation began to take place within Hinduism. Reform movements were born, which whilst breaking with orthodox Hindu ceremonial, especially as regards caste-observance, went back to the fundamental spiritual message of the ancient sages, and re-emphasized this element or that in it. The Brahmo Samaj, which rose in Bengal under the leadership of Raja Ram Mohan Roy and a succession of noble members of the Tagore family, laid emphasis on the teaching of the unity and immanence of the Divine. The Arya Samaj, which belonged to the North-west, went back to the original Vedas, the first Hindu scriptures, and gained from them the ideal of a free and radiant life for nation and local community. The Ramakrishna movement became the focus for a rapturous reawakening of the religion of Devotion: and thence was led directly into the service of the poorest and weakest. Later, there arose a variety of movements amongst the orthodox Hindus (that is, amongst those who remained punctilious in their observance of the ceremonial requirements of the caste-system). These movements constituted a recovery both of the ancient Pathway of Knowledge, in connection with a revival of interest in Hindu philosophy (Swami Vivekananda was the great leader here) and of the ancient Pathway of Deeds in connection with a new emphasis on caste-duty and caste-function. The Right Hon.

G. K. Gokhale later initiated the Servants of India Society, which stands for self-sacrificing service on behalf of the Untouchables and other unfortunates: and sends out its emissaries to render assistance whenever a great natural disaster, famine, flood or pestilence, has caused help to be needed.

For a time, about the middle of the nineteenth century, it seemed as though Macaulay's optimistic utterance, already noticed, regarding the ending of "idolatry" would be proved true. Hinduism became discredited because of the evils which had become accentuated in its vast body-politic during the "Tantric" period of the eighteenth century. Many great reformers seemed for a time about to abandon their allegiance to the ancient Hindu system, and either to become Christians or to throw up religion altogether.

Then, in the last quarter of the nineteenth century, collaterally with the first rise of Indian national feeling, there came a movement, especially associated with the name of Swami Vivekananda, for the purging of Hinduism of grossness and superstition, and for demonstrating that a man could be proud to call himself a Hindu whilst hating caste intolerance, animistic superstitions, the subjection of womanhood and other evil accretions around the Hindu system.

In our own century Mr. Gandhi, more than any other man, has come forth before the world as the representative of this point of view. But he has done much more than this. He has shown that in the heart of the Hindu tradition is a principle, variously termed Harmlessness, Soul-force, Defence of Truth (Satyagraha), Passive Resistance, which may become of first-class social and political importance for the whole world, as a method of overcoming evil without violence. Mr. Gandhi's significance is rather in the field of ethics than in that of abstract thought: but his work has been supplemented in this latter field by the teachings of the great philosopher, Professor Radhakrishnan, expressed especially in his two famous books, *The Hindu View of Life*, and *Indian Philosophy*.*

The general influence of these modern movements of thought and practice has been energetically to strip from Hinduism (at any rate as Hinduism is understood by the educated classes) the remains of superstition and social privilege. Hinduism is now shown as a religion with a message for the whole world, not only for India. Put very briefly, this message is that of the indwelling Divine life springing up in the individual soul, and making it impossible for one man to use violence against another in whom he knows this Divine life to dwell.

Opinions differ, both East and West, as to whether the modern reformers are well-advised in thus re-interpreting their religion. Many maintain that the stripping away of the rich heritage of ceremonial and picturesque belief (they naturally dislike the term superstition) has left a disembodied ghost. But none can withhold their reverence for the spirit in which the reform has been carried through, a spirit of unflinching resolve that nothing but the highest and purest that humanity can conceive of shall be left as integral to the Hindu faith.

Meanwhile amongst the mass of the people the old beliefs and practices persist, little affected by the radical purgings aloft. The temple-bells still call, melodiously. The images still are worshipped, with simple offerings. The priests still exercise a potent sway. The scriptures are still read forth. The Brahmin still strides along the street, master of all because of the majesty of his birth and the austere self-discipline of his life. Reform movements may come and go, but these things remain.

Something else remains, at the back of all the external trappings of Hindu religion, the unconquerable belief, deep in the heart of the Indian people that as a soul sows, so it shall

* London: George Allen & Unwin Ltd.

reap, and that to reap it must return. There is probably no possibility of over-stating the reactionary influence of this fundamental Hindu belief. It justifies social privilege, luxury, oppression; for it is used to interpret privilege as the result of good action in a former life: luxury as the same: and the misery of the oppressed as due to their wrong-doing heretofore. There is no chance of social justice being done in India, on anything like a scale adequate to deal with the problem of Indian poverty, till the people as a whole cease to believe in the doctrine of Return. As things are, even the most ignorant peasants hold that doctrine, with a tenacity which makes one feel the belief an elemental thing like the peasants' belief that dawn will follow the darkness of night, or that harvest will follow seedtime. In many lands corrupt religion has been the opium of the common people, but here what has to be combated is not so much religion as a fundamental world-doctrine, held alike by the profoundest philosophers and the simplest peasants.

Yet here again there are signs of hope. As we have noticed, Hinduism itself shows a variety of pathways by which Release may be attained; and the pathway followed most readily by the common people is the Pathway of Devotion. In direct personal relationship to a Saviour-God, according to the *Gita* and to a thousand other writings, the trusting soul here and now attains Release, and "returns not again." It may well be doubted whether the titanic force, which is exercised for reaction and oppression by the doctrine of Rebirth, will ever be broken except by an immense revival of the religion of Devotion; for the mind of India thinks in other-worldly and spiritual terms, even amongst the least enlightened, and it is only in such terms that an effective appeal can be made to that mind. Materialistic clap-trap has not the shadow of a chance.

In the long history of Hinduism almost all the moods of the soul which have evidenced themselves in the West are also to be found. For instance there is a school of thought whose attitude to the Divine approximates to that of Calvinism, emphasizing the necessity for passive dependence on the part of the soul in its relations to God: and there is another school declaring in opposition that the soul is called upon to make an effort of response to the divine initiative. Here the irresistible tendency to symbolism steps in (as in so many other connections); and the first school is called the "cat" school, because the mother-cat carries her kittens dangling from her mouth, whilst the opposing school is called the "monkey" school, because the baby monkey must actively cling around his mother's neck if she is to carry him safely held through the jungle! This case may illustrate how symbolism is employed in India to make clear deep spiritual things to humble minds.

One of the basic phenomena in Hindu religion is pilgrimage. Traditionally when he enters the third stage of life,* which is roughly when he holds his first grandchild on his knee, the orthodox Hindu leaves his home for ever, and becomes first an ascetic living in the forest, perhaps with a little community of pupils around him, and thereafter (in the fourth stage) a wanderer passing from one holy spot to another, eating nothing but what is given to him unasked, and staying not more than one day in each resting-place, lest he should "strike root" anywhere again. There are obvious economic and social advantages in such a tradition. The following of it means that every place of pilgrimage is thronged with great numbers of aged folk, many of them near to death. Ideally they are heedless of the sufferings and desires of the body, and intent only on acquiring the merit that shall lift them higher in the next birth, or on performing the Deeds of religion, attaining the Knowledge of the Absolute, or manifesting the Devotion to

* The first stage is that of the pupil, the second that of the householder. Each stage occupies roughly 25 years.

a Saviour-God, which shall finally absolve them from the necessity of Return.

The sight of these hosts of aged people (with many younger ones also amongst them) performing their ceremonial ablutions in a sacred river at one of the great religious festivals, convinces even the most contemptuous observer of the immense strength of Hindu religion, and of the fund of devoted self-sacrifice which exists in the Hindu heart, and which someday may be turned to the service of humanity.

XVI

ISLAM

EARLY IN THE seventh century on the occasion of the
Hejira, the Flight of Mohammed from Mecca to Medina,
which Moslems regard as the beginning of their era, the
Prophet was closely pursued by his enemies, and took refuge
with one companion in a cave. The pursuers were close at
hand, and the companion, Abu Baku, became afraid, saying
"What shall we do, who are but two against so many?"

The Prophet replied, "Say not that we are but two; for
there is a Third with us, even God."

In this unshakable faith in Divine aid, as in a number of
other ways, the founder of Islam resembles an Old Testament
prophet. The religion which he founded may be compared
with old Testament religion in various other respects. There
is the same serene and at times fanatical quality of faith; the
same detestation of making any image of God, a detestation
which springs from an overwhelming sense of the majesty and
imminence (*not* immanence) of the Divine presence, and form
a realization of the blasphemous folly of man's striving to
represent God by the work of man's own hands. There is the
same desert-joy in battle done for the cause of the Lord: the
same reliance upon a sealed and given code of revelation and
law, imparted to man directly by the Divine Will: the same
conviction that the people accepting that revelation and living by that law are a chosen and peculiar people, destined by
the Divine Will to rule the rest of mankind.

Islam stormed across the world in the seventh and eighth

centuries as a vast reforming and purifying force, sweeping before it into the limbo of oblivion a mass of corrupt accretions which had gathered around Eastern Christianity. By the time it reached India in force, however, the primitive reforming power of Islam was somewhat spent; and though great numbers of Hindus and animists were included in the fold of Islam, the main structure of Hinduism was not shaken even sufficiently to bring about any considerable movement of revolt against the universal image-worship. Islam ruled politically, but except within narrow limits never even looked like converting India as a whole to its own faith. The persecution under the Moghal Emperor Aurangzeb merely strengthened Hinduism and led to powerful reaction against Islam, led by the Maratha chieftain Sivaji. The two religions settled down into an uneasy equilibrium, side by side on the same territory.

To understand the Hindu-Moslem problem it is needful not only to realize the disastrous effects of the separate communal electorates, which have already been considered, but also the fact that distinctive religious practices of each side are fundamentally loathsome to the other. Moslem worship is of an austere character; and it goads the faithful to fury to have Hindu religious processions, led by jubilant and untuneful bands, and accompanied by ecstatic singing and shouting, advancing in a particularly leisurely manner past the mosques during worship-hours. Hindus give heartfelt adoration to the cow; and the news that on a certain festival day the local Moslems will sacrifice a cow drives Hindus into a condition of murderous rage.

In addition, there are economic difficulties. A large slice of the anti-social and grindingly oppressive money-lending in India is done by itinerant Pathan money-lenders from over the North-west frontier. They are Moslems: and their methods of extracting interest from the Hindu peasantry are summary and drastic. The hatred which their cruelty arouses is extended to embrace all Moslems, especially in rural districts where other Moslems are few and far between.

Again, in districts where there is a large Moslem population, the energetic teachings of Islam against usury can be enforced, and as agricultural loans are an elemental necessity under present conditions in India, the money-lending falls into the hands of immigrant Hindus or Jains (members of an early reform movement within Hinduism, which demanded the abolition of animal sacrifices). Hence arises communal friction, the solution of which is clearly an energetic central pushing of the movement for agricultural cooperation, and especially for cooperative credit banks, which will render the money-lender unnecessary.

Islam has succeeded, where Christianity and the other great religions have failed, in creating an effective and equal brotherhood of believers. This does not of course mean that either political democracy or economic socialism are characteristic of Islam. Far from it. But it does mean that there is among Moslems a general sense that all men, high as well as low, rich as well as poor, are equal in nothingness before the greatness of God. The Emperor worships by the side of the beggar in the mosque. From Morocco to Java, and from China to Zanzibar, Moslems are all blood-brothers, owning the same holy book, written in the same sacred Arabic language—the language of the mind of God—and bowing in prayer towards the same holy spot, at Mecca.

It is hard for us Christians, divided on the religious side into numerous denominations, and on the social and economic side into competing classes, to comprehend how mighty a bond is this brotherhood of Islam. Its strength may be illustrated from the complete naturalness and unashamedness with which Moslems everywhere practise their religion. At a football match one may see the Moslem students amongst the spectators turn away from the touchline, as the sun sets, and going a few paces back, there perform the elaborate genuflections of the evening prayer, with complete self-possession and lack of embarrassment. It is the same in the public parks all over India. The postures adopted during the moments of prayer are striking, especially in the utter abandonment of abasement before God which they typify. They are also energetically varied, the worshipper flinging himself from time to time on his face. The Westerner is struck with amazement at the lack of self-consciousness with which the ritual is followed. A friend of mine, in London, who had been able to be of service to a Moslem student, one evening found her private office borrowed, without permission asked, as a suitable place for the performing of these prayers!

This ritual of prayer symbolizes the extraordinary strength of the tie which binds all Moslems together. They are the same prayers, the same postures, everywhere. They denote the same act of conscious individual self-abasement before the greatness and grandeur of God. Obviously they are nothing to be ashamed of, but rather a battle-flag to be borne high, a confession of world-shaking faith, and a symbol of world-conquering unity. The average Western Christian shrinks in shame from any outward confessing of his faith. The Moslem glories in the opportunity to acclaim the world-brotherhood of the people of Allah.

This pan-Islamic brotherhood has political results, which we have already noticed. A rapidly growing proportion of the Moslems in India feel that their primary allegiance is not to what they regard as the merely geographical expression "India," but to the Islamic brotherhood. For this reason they desire, in the first place, separate communal electorates for Moslems in the new organization of Indian democracy: then, a separate Moslem State in India, composed of those provinces in which there is a Moslem majority, however small, in the total population, together with some at least of the Indian States which are ruled by Moslem princes: next, they want a pan-Islamic federation between this Indian "Pakistan" (holy land of the Moslems) and Islamic states outside India, e.g., Afghanistan, Iran, Iraq, Saudi Arabia, Transjordania, perhaps Egypt, Palestine, Syria, Turkey, and others.

We have already recognized the fact that any foreign imperialism is forced to find privileged groups in the conquered country, by whose aid it can govern the rest, and is bound to foster and protect these privileged groups. In India it has not only been by the aid of the princes, and of the rich land-owners and (later) capitalists, that we have governed. It has also been by the aid of the Moslems. They had held the last great Indian Empire before our coming. They were a strongly self-conscious minority-element in most parts of the country; and generally speaking they stood in a privileged economic position as a relic of the Moghal domination. Almost automatically therefore they came to be our allies and helpers vis-à-vis the great mass of the Hindu population. The Moslems were comparatively slow in coming to an appreciation of the advantages of Western education, as fitting them to take a share in the profitable task of aiding British imperialism govern India; but of recent years they have insisted successfully on being given a percentage of public appointments proportionate rather to their numbers than to their intellectual equipment.

It is of fundamental importance that the British control, before it releases its hold on India, should make up its mind whether in the long perspectives of history it will be doing right in encouraging the Moslems, as was done in the Cripps proposals of 1942, to look forward to the establishment of a separate Moslem State in India, entirely independent of "Hindustan" (the provinces with a majority of Hindus), staffed by the Moslem officials already trained in our public services, and eventually to be federated with the other Moslem states of the Near East.*

It can be predicted with absolute certainty that if independence is given on these terms to India (or rather to Pakistan-plus-Hindustan, for the term India will have become meaningless), there will be speedy and ferocious civil war. The fruit of British rule will be seen to be divisions even more disastrous than were the divisions at the time when that control was first established.

It must be insisted at this point, however, that by no means all Indian Moslems believe in Pakistan. In 1942 the President of the Indian National Congress was a Moslem; and there were many thousands of Indian Moslems in the Congress ranks. They are in a difficult position, especially in view of the strength of the Islamic brotherhood; for they always lie open to the taunt that they love India better than Islam; and in the East, where religion and politics are not divorced, as with us, but are integrally united, such a taunt is far more damaging than we can estimate.

Especially in the North-west there has been for a number of years a growing movement for the spiritualizing and purging of Islam. The primitive ferocity of the desert has been toned down. Such awkward points as the Prophet's domestic arrangements or the sensuous delights of Paradise have been allegorized. New editions of the holy book, the *Koran*, have been produced, into which these new-fangled explanations have been introduced; and in general the modern critical faculty has been let loose upon the foundations of Islamic religion. Whether the faith can stand up against such a process, and can emerge from it stronger and purer, has yet

---

* The Sikhs are now (1942) showing signs of following the lead of the Moslems in demanding separate and independent statehood for their community. There have been many signs of the Depressed Classes doing the same! Along this pathway nothing is to be found but national dismemberment. Balkanization and civil warfare.

to be seen. The reform movement has met with tremendous opposition, extending even to the infliction of martyrdom, at the hands of forces of literalism and of reactionary tradition. But it must never be forgotten how radical a reformation has taken place in Turkish Islam within the last twenty years. As the home of the Caliph Turkey was for centuries the centre of Islamic prestige; and it is inevitable that sooner or later the influence of what has happened there will have its effect in India. Now the main significance of the reform-movement in Turkish Islam has been to divorce politics and religion. The Caliphate has disappeared, and with it the reactionary influence of the Moslem clergy on state affairs. Meanwhile the position of womanhood has been immensely improved, a widespread system of education has been introduced, and thereby the numbing and enervating effect of the Islamic belief in Fate (Kismat) has been shaken.

Sooner or later the same type of reform movement will take place in India. That day should be hastened by a concentrated effort to spread popular education amongst the mass of the ninety-four million Indian Moslems. Their women are still largely in seclusion, and abysmally ignorant; and the men still tend to sink nervelessly under any disaster with the words, "It is the will of Allah." The real hope of the future, in regard to this complex and menacing problem of the position of the Moslems in a free India, lies in the realm of rightly devised education on a sufficiently extended scale. Such education will loosen the stranglehold of reactionary religion on political and national life.

Probably the greatest single contribution made by Islam to India has been in the realm of art. Even the most casual visitor has felt the influence of the chaste purity of line and decoration in the great Islamic buildings in the North, especially at Agra and Delhi. In music and poetry also great things have been done by Indian Moslems; and the whole world will some day acknowledge its indebtedness to the teachings of Mohammedan mysticism, naturalized in India, though coming originally from Persia.

But great as these Islamic contributions are to India and to the body-politic of humanity, the greatest of all Islamic gifts is the object-lesson which the "House of Islam" (the whole Islamic world) offers in the power of religion to transcend all barriers of race, colour, caste or nationality, in one universal brotherhood. This is what Christianity should be, and should do: but is not, and does not do. All honour, in this regard, to the Moslems: and may we swiftly begin to learn from them.

XVII

THE BRITISH SYSTEM

ABOUT THREE HUNDRED AND TWENTY YEARS before Christ the Greek traveller Megasthemes recorded this about the India of his day:—"The village communities are republics which are almost independent of any outside relations." In 1819 the great British administrator Mountstuart Elphinstone said the same:—"The village communities contain in miniature all the materials of a State within themselves . . . They are an excellent remedy for the imperfections of a bad government."

In 1830 another great Englishman, Sir Charles Metcalfe, wrote as follows:—"The village communities are little Republics, having nearly everything that they want within themselves, and almost independent of any foreign relations. Dynasty after dynasty tumbles down; revolution succeeds to revolution; Hindu, Pathan, Moghal, Mahratta, Sikh, English are masters in turn; but the village community remains the same. In time of trouble they arm and fortify themselves: a hostile army passes through the country; the village community collect their cattle within their walls, and let the enemy pass. The union of the village communities, each one forming a separate little State in itself, has, I conceive, contributed more than any other cause to the preservation of the people of India through all revolutions and changes, and it is in a high degree conducive to their happiness and to the enjoyment of a great portion of freedom and independence. I wish therefore that the village communities may never be disturbed, and dread everything that has a tendency to break them up."

Even as late as 1864 as acute an observer as Sir John Lawrence declared, "The village communities, each of which is a little republic, are the most abiding of Indian institutions."

Yet one result of the working of the British system has been in large measure to destroy this intensely valuable thing. In the words of a later English administrator, Sir Henry Cotton, "a costly and mechanical centralization has taken the place of the former system of local self-government and local arbitration."

Side by side with this disaster, the break-up of village autonomy, has come that steady increase of poverty to which we have already given some attention. It was already noticed by Bishop Heber in 1826, when he said, "The peasantry in the Company's provinces are on the whole worse off, poorer, and more dispirited, than the subjects of the Native Princes." The matter was expressed about a century later by the following extract from a South Indian economic survey:—

Puman, Panchama (Untouchable): He has seven in his family, himself, his father, wife and four children. Owns a mud house of one room and a veranda for his large family. He has 13 pigs. He works as a coolie, building mud houses, transplanting paddy, digging graves for the dead. His work is very irregular, and as for wages they may average about three rupees per month (say four shillings and sixpence). In actual wages he may not get more than Rs. 35 to Rs. 40 (say £3) in a whole year. In harvest time he gets gifts of grain. The dead cattle go to him. He eats the flesh no matter of what disease the animal died. He sells the skins. At marriages and festivals he gets gifts of food. He lives a miserable, animal existence from hand to mouth, and has only one meal a day.* He has a debt of Rs. 10 with nothing to pay it. There are a hundred such families in this little village. Their condition is deplorable, with no prospect of improvement.

Not only was there no prospect of improvement; but a few years after this survey was made, the depression was to

* Sir William Hunter declared many years ago that 40 million people in India pass through life on one meal a day.

cause the rural population of India to become catastrophically poorer. According to one authority the average net income of a Punjab farmer fell from ninepence per day in 1928–9 to three farthings a day in 1930–1. The annual consumption of sugar fell from 7.7 lbs. per head in 1930 to 5.8 in 1932. The consumption of cloth per head was 13¼ yards per annum in 1913, and 9½ in 1930.

It may be noted in regard to the above survey that Puman was by no means the poorest of the Indian poor; for he owned his house, he had 13 pigs and (marvellous to say) his debt was only Rs. 10.

Along with this ever-increasing poverty has gone a degeneration in standards of civilization, as shown by the great recent increase in the number of child-marriages. Dr. Eleanor Rathbone's examination of the census statistics has shown that there were over six million more child husbands and wives in 1931 than in 1921; and that wives under the age of five quadrupled in numbers between the same dates. This was in spite of the Sarda Act of 1927 aimed at making child-marriage illegal. Dr. Rathbone records how young girls often die in agony after many days of fruitless labour: and she speaks of a girl of 21 who had already had seven children, and who did not attempt to recover after her last confinement, saying, "It is no use, because maternity comes on every year." There are two hundred thousand deaths in childbirth every year. The increase in child-marriage, with its attendant evils, is mainly caused by the increasing poverty, which brings upon parents the need of getting daughters provided for early. In Japan they sell the girls to the factories.

The break-up of the primitive village polity has thus been accompanied by increasing poverty and by lowered standards of civilization.

We must realize that the British System began badly. A House of Commons Report of 1773 alleged that from 1757 to

1765 bribes to European officials in India amounted to two million pounds. Macaulay believed that this corruption was largely the cause of the dreadful famine in Bengal in 1770, in the course of which, though one-third of the population died, the revenue was actually increased, by methods which will not bear examination. Sheridan declared in the House of Commons in 1787 that Warren Hastings had received a bribe of £100,000 for the Treaty of Chunar: and he summed up the administration of the East India Company by saying, "They wield a truncheon with one hand and pick a pocket with the other."

In 1813 Sir Thomas Munro declared that the East India Company's servants placed Indian weavers under guard till they promised to work for the Company only; then a subordinate Indian official was placed to beat them with a cane if they were slow with deliveries, and the weaver had to pay his salary!

In 1857 Richard Cobden said, "The entire scheme of our Indian rule is based on the assumption that the natives will be willing instruments of their own humiliation." J. S. Mill called that rule, "the most complete despotism that could possibly exist." John Bright said, "the Indian Services are a vast department of outdoor relief for the British upper classes."

It is to be noticed that in the period of railway construction many Indian lines had their losses made good and the interest on their stock guaranteed by Government, although the shareholders were responsible to no one. Hence came wild extravagance, and huge profits to English stockholders.

In the terrible famine-year 1897 ten million pounds worth of grain was exported to England.

Again, the Indian taxpayer has been forced to pay the cost of all the wars by which England has conquered his country. India was even forced to pay the cost of the Abyssinian

war of 1867, about which Sir Charles Trevelyan declared
before a Parliamentary Committee in 1876, "India was in no
way more concerned with our expedition to Abyssinia than
were Australia and Canada . . . The only reason why we
did not make a similar demand from Australia and Canada to
help pay the expenses of that war was that we knew perfectly
well that they would indignantly scout such a proposal."
India was also made to pay two-thirds of the cost of the
Egyptian war of 1882. In all during the nineteenth century it
has been reckoned that the British Government conducted
111 wars, raids and military expeditions for which the
abysmally poor Indian taxpayer had to pay.

Incidentally it is recorded that one Indian Prince spent
£115,000 on entertaining one Viceroy, and £200,000 on entertaining another: and that another Prince spends nine times
as much on his motor cars as upon education in his State.

There is an unpleasantly commercial odour, even to-day,
about our whole system in India. The well-known indiffer-
ence of the House of Commons to Indian affairs was explained
as follows not long ago by a Member of Parliament: "When
the shareholders fail to turn up at a meeting, it indicates
approval of the policy being pursued." A distinguished English administrator spoke in 1919 of "our duty to the one
thousand million pounds worth of British capital invested in
India." Some great jute mills near Calcutta paid an annual
dividend of 125 per cent. from 1918 to 1928. In 1928 five jute
companies in Bengal were paying over 100 per cent., but in
spite of this the management decided to increase working
hours from 54 to 60 and to reduce pay. In 1923 a coal firm
paid 150 per cent.; but in some mines women were getting
the equivalent of fivepence a day. It has been reckoned by a
prominent economist that every fifth man in Great Britain,
is dependent, either directly or indirectly, on our Indian connection for his livelihood. Another authority declared in 1930

that four shillings in the pound of our national revenue comes from the profits which Great Britain draws from her commercial relations with India.

This aspect of our connection with India may be summed up in the words used by Sir William Joynson Hicks in the House of Commons in 1926:—"We did not conquer India for the good of the Indians—that is cant. We conquered India by the sword, and by the sword we shall hold it. I am not such a hypocrite as to say that we hold India for the benefit of the Indians. We hold it as the finest outlet for British goods in general and for Lancashire goods in particular."

In 1880 Lord Roberts wrote from Kabul, with singular clarity of vision:—"It may not be flattering to our *amour propre*, but I feel sure I am right when I say that the less the Afghans see of us, the less will they dislike us!"

The same is emphatically true of India herself!

The British have performed great services on India's behalf, especially in the establishment of internal peace, the development of communications, the fighting of famine, and the introduction of an educational system which, however inadequate and mis-conceived, has still given India national consciousness and national aspirations. But at the same time these glaring facts stand out, increasing poverty, demoralization (as shown by the growth of child-marriage), the flowing of vast masses of wealth from India to England, and (last but not least) the necessity of using odious forms of violence in order to keep the system running. Even at the beginning of this century, under Lord Curzon, the Report of the Police Commission, published by the Government itself, contained these words: "The police force is far from efficient; it is defective in training; it is inadequately supervised; it is generally regarded as corrupt and oppressive; and it has utterly failed to secure the confidence and cordial cooperation of the people." A generation later, in 1931, there were 6,189 official whippings (i.e., cases of infliction of torture by the police).* During the previous year the martial law regulations put into force at Sholapur threatened with five years' imprisonment anyone not declaring his knowledge or reasonable belief that any of his relatives or dependants had joined in some recent disorders: and four boys aged fifteen were flogged (one with fifteen strokes of the birch) for breaking this and similar regulations. The Bengal Ordinance of 1931 sanctioned collective fining, and instituted special tribunals of three members to try offenders in secret and empowered to condemn them to death or to imprisonment for life, without appeal and in the absence of the accused, by a majority vote of two judges to one.

Mr. Ramsay Macdonald, late Prime Minister of Great Britain, declared rightly, in his book on *The Government of India*, that "a power of repression habitually enjoyed tends to develop a habit of mind in the government, which regards all effectively troublesome criticism as sedition." He put things even more pungently in his *Awakening of India*:— "The Indian Civil Service has sought to widen the scope of sedition until it should include everything not flattery." It is noteworthy that Ramsay Macdonald's two books were banned in India even when he was himself Prime Minister!

There is only one cure for this situation, freedom for India, and in preparation for that freedom the widest possible extension of a rightly-devised system of popular education. But let it be repeated that both the freedom and the education must be made applicable to the population of the Indian States, as well as to British India. Otherwise freedom for India will be impossible.

* Late in 1942 news was let through the Government censorship to the effect that the Indian police had been beating schoolgirls.

XVIII

GAUTAMA THE BUDDHA

GAUTAMA THE BUDDHA ("the Enlightened One") lived probably from about 560 to about 480 B.C. That is, he belonged to, and was the brightest jewel of, the wonderful age which produced, contemporaneously in totally unrelated quarters of the world, Confucius and the scheme of ethics which still rules in China, the fullest perfection of pre-Christian Judaism in the Second Isaiah, and the ideal democracy of Cleisthenes in Athens, with its extraordinary flowering of literary genius in the drama, lyric poetry, history, and philosophy.

The Buddha is the greatest of all Indians; and it is to be noted that his greatness, and his contribution to world-thought and world-civilization does not lie in that realm of abstract philosophy which is generally regarded as the peculiar Indian gift to mankind. As has been pointed out again and again in recent years, and notably in Rudolf Otto's invaluable book *India's Religion of Grace,* such a view is tragically unjust. The dominant element in Indian religion has for many ages regarded the monistic philosophy of the Vedanta as "a vile and pestilent heresy": and has taught Release from re-birth through personal dependence on a personal Saviour-God. This dominant element, the Pathway of Devotion, leads us straight back to the Buddha.

It is true that Gautama disclaimed all knowledge about God, and that he founded a religion which strictly speaking was originally atheistic. But what matters about Gautama in this connection, is not what he taught, but what he was. His

personality burst through the trammels of his teachings: and
to such effect that, within a few generations of his death; men
were worshipping Gautama himself as God, and had learnt
from the memories of his merciful and loving personality to
believe that these same moral qualities are at the centre of
the universe. From this fountain-head sprang the tradition of
Devotion (*Bhakti*). It is a strongly theistic tradition; yet it
goes back to a teacher known to all future generations as the
Illuminated One, who humbly forbore to claim any authority
or illumination enabling him to give any teaching at all about
God. He was redemptive in his life, with the result that
countless millions of human souls have come to believe, flatly
against this man's own teachings, in a God whose character
and activity is like Gautama's.

Gautama is the ideal embodiment of the type of character
which is admired most by the soul of India. He is so because
he has himself made India admire that type of character, and
because he has made India demand that type of character in
God also. India has said, not only "Gautama must be God,"
but also "God must be at least as good as Gautama." And all
this in spite of the fact that the organized religion called
Buddhism faded out of India nearly a thousand years ago!
These things require earnest consideration.

Gautama embodies the best of Indian moral and spiritual
idealism in a personality which is the permanent norm of
the four great Indian virtues—in a personality so remarkable
that it has taught a vast world-culture that God also must be
the permanent norm of those four great virtues. These characteristic Indian virtues, which form the contribution of India
to the ethical treasure-house of humanity, are pity, self-
sacrifice, loving and redemptive harmlessness, and the conquest of selfish desire. Pity, for the world's need and pain;
self-sacrifice as meaning the renunciation of all that the world
holds dear in order to meet that need and conquer that pain:

loving and redemptive harmlessness, since evil is conquered by good-will and not by more evil; the conquest of selfish desire, since the world can only be saved from evil and pain as we get our minds off ourselves, with our individual profit, and on to the needs of others.

It is perhaps well to observe that in studying the Buddha, as in studying other Indian matters, one should resolve to search for and emphasize the best that can be found in him and his system. We shall not imitate the flies that go straight to a raw wound, and make it worse!

Gautama was born the son of a Prince, and was brought up in every kind of comfort and luxury. His father, noticing the boy's sensitive nature, sought to fence him off from any opportunity of seeing anything painful, by keeping him within a park and a palace surrounded by high walls, which the soldiers or guard forbade him to pass. At last his father reluctantly consented to let him go forth for one short drive in his chariot to see his capital city. He saw an old man, and returned to his palace and his lovely young bride filled with a first impression of the world's pain. On a subsequent occasion, in spite of his father's strenuous endeavours to ensure that during Gautama's short progress through the city he should see no disturbing sight, he met a sick man. Later on, he saw a dead man being carried to the burning ghat.

After this third vision of the meaning of the world's pain, Gautama said farewell to his wife and infant child, escaped from his palace by night, and became a wandering ascetic, seeking everywhere, and for a time through dark penances and self-tormentings, for the secret by which he could help mankind to escape from pain and sorrow. At last Illumination came to him; and he preached through the rest of his long life, by example as well as by precept, the Four Noble Truths. He founded also the Buddhist *Sanga*, or Fellowship, which is essentially an ascetic order dedicated to the carrying forward of the task of proclaiming in word and action the Four Noble Truths.

What are these Four Noble Truths?

The first is, that *there is Pain*. We must beware of living in a fool's paradise, of going through life in a self-centred or dilettante spirit, content to ignore the fact that a very large proportion of our fellow-denizens of the earth go to bed each night hungry, that they suffer wrong and oppression, that there are wars and famines and epidemics of pestilence. Gautama set out to destroy the possibility of other people being brought up as he had been, like ostriches with their heads buried in the sand. Facts must be faced; and the big revelant fact with regard to man's position on this earth is that he suffers. It must be realized also that to Gautama and his Sanga the recognition of the world's suffering was a battle-cry to action, bidding them share the pain in order to relieve it. As they realized the significance of the First Noble Truth these early Buddhists forsook all that they had, came down redemptively into the midst of the pain, took the worst of it upon themselves, and strove to lighten the burden of their fellowmen.

Secondly, *Pain is caused by self-regarding Desire:* or in our modern jargon egotism in some form or another (e.g., in the form of thirst for power or profits) is at the heart of the problem of the world's pain. Gautama's answer to the mother who had lost her child is well known. He bade her go from house to house till she should find a home where death had never been. Her search was vain, whereupon he showed her that her own pain was but a tiny part of the universal destiny of pain. This response has often been stigmatized as cold and unsympathetic, but such a judgment is superficial. Gautama knew that most grief is egocentric. We feel resentfully that *we* have been unjustly deprived of something *we* loved: our acquisitive instincts are outraged; so is our self-esteem. **We** look forward to long years of *our own* loneliness: we think of all that the loved one might have been and have done *for us*. The way to conquer such egotistic grief is to rise above egotism: and the way to do that is to realize that other people suffer, and to sink one's own suffering is the effort to relieve their suffering. So also with other forms of pain. A pure unselfishness will turn any tragedy coming upon oneself personally, into a means of grace for other people.

Gautama is therefore right also in his Third Noble Truth, *Get rid of self-regarding Desire, and you will get rid of Pain*. We all of us know cases—they are particularly common perhaps in war-time—in which fear and suffering have been swallowed up, or rather transfigured out of all recognition, as the sufferer has concentrated his attention and his activity on a cause beyond himself, or on the needs of other persons. This is true even if the body has been so immobilized by suffering that the only form of activity which can be undertaken is that of the soul. Such sufferers will say, "Don't worry about me, get on with the job," or "Help that other fellow." Their pain has become a radiant incentive to redemptive good-will.

The *Fourth Noble Truth* is perhaps less satisfactory *To conquer self-regarding Desire, you must follow the path of Righteousness*. Gautama specifies eight types of righteousness which are to be followed, right faith, right feelings, right livelihood, right effort, right contemplation, right thinking, right speaking, right action. Such advice clearly does little more than throw the problem of the conquest of egotism one stage farther back. It brings us up against the problem of *how* to be righteous in thought, action, speech, and so forth. A reinforcement of the will is obviously needed; but it is not directly apparent how this reinforcement is to come about. Gautama's followers have realized the difficulty, and have answered the problem by substituting in effect another for their Master's Fourth Noble Truth. They have said, and their advice has been more practical than his, "Follow Gautama; worship Gautama; model your life on Gautama; and you shall find your will so reinforced that you can conquer the self-regarding Desire which is in you, and is the cause of your own pain and of your failure to minister redemptively to the world's pain."

Many Buddhists have gone farther still, and have developed the doctrine of the Eternal Buddha, constantly reborn in holy souls. They have thought of their Master as for ever refusing to enter the final blessed state of Nirvana, the loss of all consciousness of individuality, in order that he may continue to help needy souls to conquer pain and egotism.

It is here that the connection is most clearly evident between Buddhist Devotion and the long subsequent history of the Hindu school of Release by Devotion. A few centuries after Buddha the matter was put in immortal words by the author of the *Gita*. The speaker is Krishna, the charioteer of the soul, incarnation of the Supreme God:—

Whenever there is decay of righteousness, and exaltation of unrighteousness, then I Myself come forth: for the protection of the righteous, for the destruction of evil-doers, for the sake of firmly establishing righteousness, I am born from age to age. He who thus knoweth My divine birth and activity, in its essence, when he abandoneth the body, cometh not to birth again, but cometh unto Me.

In this memorable passage the *Gita* effectually welcomed into Hindusim the Buddhist teaching of Devotion, and installed Buddha himself as the leader of a long line of redemptive personalities.

It will be well for us to consider some of the main sources of the Buddhist teaching concerning the overcoming of evil by good-will, teaching which has had incalculable influence on India, and notably in our own day on the thought and activities of Mr. Gandhi.

"Hatred does not cease by hatred at any time; hatred ceases by love" (actual words of Gautama: *Dhammapada*, I, 5).

"If you are attacked with fists, with stones, with sticks, with swords, you must still refuse all resentment, and preserve a loving mind with no secret spite. Your good-will should be as inexhaustible as the waters of the Ganges." (*Majjhima*, 21.)

"For all alike your love should be one and the same in its nature, and should include all realms, all beings, and all ages. . . . Make no difference between those who are friendly, indifferent or hostile to you." (*Majjhima*, 103.)

"Kindly thought is the best kind of retaliation."

"Ye monks, if robbers and murderers should sever your joints and limbs with a saw, he who fell into anger thereat would not be fulfilling my instructions."

"A king's son, Kunala, had both his eyes put out through the malice of his stepmother. When, with collected mind, after the first eye had been torn out, he had it put into his hand by the executioner, as he held it and looked at it with his remaining eye, suddenly true knowledge arose in him, and throwing off every feeling of *I*, he broke out with the exulting words: 'May she long enjoy life, power and happiness who has made use of this means in order to make me a participator in this great boon'."

"A monk named Purna wished to settle in a land whose inhabitants were noted for their violence. 'If they abuse and injure thee, what shalt thou think?' said the Buddha to him. 'I shall then think, "These people are really good in that they only abuse me, but do not beat me and throw stones at me".' 'But if they beat thee and throw stones at thee?' 'Then I shall think, "They are really good in that they only beat me and throw stones at me, but do not attack me with sticks and swords".' 'But if they attack thee with sticks and sword?' 'Then I shall think, "They are really good in that they do not rob me of life outright".' 'But if they rob thee of life?' 'Then

I shall think, "These people are really good to me in that they have freed me from the burden of this life".' Whereupon the Buddha said, 'Well hast thou spoken, Purna. Go and deliver, thou self-deliverer! Lead to the other shore, thou that hast thyself reached that shore! Comfort, thou that art already comforted! Guide to Nirvana, thou that art already entered into Nirvana!'." (*Majjhima*, 145.)

XIX

BHAKTI

AT THE SACK of Delhi, in 1857, an Indian ascetic, sitting in contemplation, was bayoneted by a British soldier. As he received his death wound, the ascetic looked up at his slayer, with the words, "Thou too art He." The typical religion of India is generally regarded in the West as an undifferentiated mysticism; the whole effort of the seeking soul is to realize its entire oneness with the Absolute, in whom all other souls are potentially also one. The dying ascetic's words may be taken as typical of this attitude. But in India itself there has been waged, literally for thousands of years, the hottest of battles against this "monistic" mysticism; and in opposition to it, as we have already noticed, there has arisen a fervent witness to the reality of Divine Grace, which is to be apprehended in devotion to a personal Saviour-God. In the thought of many of the greatest saints in India this Way of Devotion has been the sole and unique pathway to God.

The greatest of the monistic teachers, Shankara, taught about the year 800 that there is only a single genuine reality, Brahman, and that nothing else exists, the seen universe being mere illusion (*maya*) existing only in the minds of those who live in ignorance. He taught also that there can be no sort of personal relation to Brahman, such as love or reverence, for "he is beyond the triplicity of knower, known and knowing"; there is only one possible relation to him, that of complete identity, which cannot properly be called a relation at all, for where there is only identity there can be no relationship.

There are still numerous deeply philosophic saints and thinkers in India who follow Shankara's Way of Knowledge of identity with Brahman; but the heart of India is with the Bhakti revolt against that Way of Knowledge and towards the Way of Devotion. We have already noticed that the greatest single document of Bhakti is the *Gita;* and vast numbers of Indians, especially quite ordinary and busy people, would re-echo the words of Mr. Gandhi:—"When disappointment stares me in the face, and all alone I see no one ray of light, I go back to the *Gita.* I find a verse here and a verse there, and I immediately begin to smile in the midst of overwhelming tragedies. . . . My life has been full of external tragedies; and if they have left no visible, no indelible scar on me, I owe it all to the teachings of the *Gita.*"

As we have seen, Bhakti goes back, historically, far beyond the *Gita* to Gautama; but in such a verse as this (*Gita,* xviii, 64), the full Bhakti message comes home to India:—

Direct thy mind to Me, love Me, sacrifice for Me, honour Me; thus wilt thou come to Me; this I promise thee solemnly. Thou art dear to Me. . . . Find thy refuge in Me alone.

There is the insistence also that devotion to the Saviour-God must bear fruit in a pitiful and merciful attitude of life towards the misery of the world, (in view of the prevailing thought-mould of Transmigration, this teaching is as revolutionary as the Buddha's insistence upon compassionate goodwill). For example, a famous saint of the Bhakti school declares,

There is a sign by which one can know whether a man is religious or not. If a misfortune befalls another, notice whether thy heart is moved with sympathy for him or not, whether it suffers pain with him or the opposite. In the former case thou mayst be certain that thou art in filial relation with God, in the latter that He rejects thee.

Many of the Bhakti saints give expression to an intense rapture of devotion towards the object of their worship, a rapture so intense that one Western scholar describes India as a God-intoxicated country. A classical definition declares that, "by Bhakti we mean an intense love of God. Love of God is like the food of immortals, for it makes a man perfect, deathless and satisfied. A man who has once experienced such love will see that alone, hear that alone, and speak that alone; for he ever thinks of that alone."

The great Bhakti teacher, Tulsi Das, who translated the ancient epic, the *Ramayana*, into Hindi, making it a vivid and fundamental document of his faith, tells how a philosopher who was learned in the monistic scriptures began to recite to him once about the Absolute Reality, formless, infinite, impersonal, invisible, incomprehensible. But the poet begged the philosopher to cease, crying, "Sir, show us the Incarnate." To such thinkers and poets as Tulsi Das the monistic doctrines destroyed the possibility of everything that gave meaning to salvation, above all the possibility of the enjoyment of God. To the followers of Bhakti, salvation must of necessity involve personal consciousness, or how could one love God? and the relationship between lover and loved must be real, not merely a form of self-deception; for their root idea was that God loves mankind and thirsts for the response of man's love.

The modern poet Rabindranath Tagore is in the main stream of Bhakti thought when he says:—"Our Master himself hath taken upon him the bonds of creation. He is bound in our midst for ever." For the Bhakti thinkers hold that God is not content to dwell aloof and separate, in an easy heaven; but that he comes to earth in self-identifying and redemptive activity on behalf of the poor and needy; and this is why the saints love him.

The greatest of all the Bhakti poets was probably Tukaram,

who was born in Western India in 1608. He was a peasant,
and a Sudra, a low-caste man. He was bitterly persecuted by
the Brahmins; but became the chief figure of the Maratha
literary renaissance, and was invited to his court by the great
Maratha chieftain, Sivaji. He wrote in an irregular rhymed
metre, with great force and naïveté, and with remarkable
conciseness, so that a typical stanza, containing only twenty-
two words in the original, needs sixty-four for translation into
English. He places a stern emphasis on the need for purity of
life, and ′dependence on God's grace. Tukaram's songs are
still widely sung by the peasants in Western India. Typical
poems may be thus translated:—

(1) Lord, I have abandoned all for Thee,
     Yet evermore Desire riseth in my heart,
     And maketh me forget Thy love;

     Ah, save me, save me,
     Save me by Thyself;

     As thus I bow before Thee, Lord,
     Come, dwell within,
     Live Thou Thy secret life in me,
     And save me by Thyself.

(2) Thee, Thee alone, O God,
     My soul desireth;

     No gaudy Heaven I seek,
     No bottomless absorption in the Absolute;

     Life in this world of death is good, is all I need,
     For I have Thee;

     All men shall know it, Lord—
     I am Thy servant, Thee I love, and Thee adore.

(3) Thou, O Saviour-God,
     Art all the life that I have ever truly lived;

Thou, O Saviour-God,
Art all my merit;

Thou, O Saviour-God,
Art all the store of righteousness I bring to Thee;

Thou, O Saviour-God,
Art all my faithfulness to duty,
Art all my loyalty to daily vows;

O Thou Beloved of my soul,
O Thou, who art all love, all grace, all goodness.
Speak to me now Thy word of peace.

Or, in another form:—"Where pity, pardon, peace abide, there God dwells; thither He hastens to make His home, for spirit is the place of His abiding, and where these graces have free play, He tarries."

In our own time the great Indian Christian poet, Narayan Vaman Tilak, has declared, "As for myself, it was over the bridge of Tukaram's verse that I came to Christ." Tilak has shown that the devotional poetry of Tukaram, and of the Bhakti school generally, is a *preparatio evangelica* of the greatest significance and value. At the age of 55 this thoroughly non-Westernized Indian Christian relinquished all means of support and, with his wife, took up the life of a wandering devotee. He said, "Henceforth I must be free of all human agencies, except in love and service, and must be bound entirely and for all purposes to Christ and the Gospel. . . . I am a Christian devotee, which means a follower of Love, never of Detachment or Absorption, and I will try to be and to do as I am led by the Spirit of God."

Tilak's poems, like those of Tukaram, breathe a rapturous delight in the presence of the Lord; but there is this great difference, the Lord is Christ, not Krishna as Krishna is understood by the Maratha peasant. When N. V. Tilak cries,

> From this day onward Thou art mine,
> Brother beloved and King divine,
> From this day on.

he seems to be building directly on the conceptions of his great forerunner; but the difference in conception of the character and nature of the Divine Comrade and Friend must never be forgotten.

To the follower of Bhakti religion the state of full vision of the Beloved of his soul is called *Samadhi*. Contemplation culminates in this ecstatic experience, whose glories numerous poets and saints have endeavoured in vain to describe. This ideal also has been inherited and brought into Indian Christianity by Tilak and other Christian devotees, amongst whom the most notable of recent years has been Sadhu Sundar Singh. I well remember my first meeting with the Sadhu. I had been staying in a minute hill-village sixty miles into the mountains behind Simla. One morning word was brought to me that a Christian Sadhu (devotee) had arrived at another village, fifteen hundred feet down the mountain-side, from Tibet. I ran down to see him: and for hours listened enormously interested to his accounts of his spiritual experiences and of his missionary journeys in Tibet. He was by birth a Sikh of the Punjab. When a boy, he had been bitterly opposed to Christianity, and falling into despair had decided to commit suicide. The night previously he tried to pray. In his own words, "At 4:30 a.m. I saw a great light in the room where I was praying . . . Then as I prayed and looked into the light, I saw the form of the Lord Jesus Christ. It had such an appearance of glory and love! . . . I felt that a vision like this could not come out of my own imagination. I heard a voice saying in Hindustani, 'How long will you persecute me? I have come to save you; you were praying to know the right way. Why do you not take it?' So I fell at His feet and got this wonderful peace, which I could not get anywhere else. This was the joy I was wishing to get. This was heaven itself. When I got up, the vision had disappeared; but although the vision disappeared, the peace and joy have remained with me ever since."

This was the beginning of a lifetime of extraordinary power and attractiveness. The Sadhu became famous all over India, and far beyond.* He suffered greatly during his constant missionary journeys, and never returned from his last expedition to Tibet, undertaken in 1929; but everyone who came in contact with him was impressed by the fashion in which his personality and his utterances interpreted Christ to India in terms which the age-long tradition of Bhakti religion enabled India to understand.

A typical saying of the Sadhu's was this:—"From my fourteen years' experience as a Sadhu for Jesus Christ I can say with confidence that the Cross will bear those who bear the Cross, until it lifts them up to heaven, into the presence of their Saviour."

India finds it hard to understand or to love a Western religion which comes to her joined with Western imperialism, taught by men in Western garb and with white faces, who live on a standard often far above that even of her own middle class. From time immemorial the man of religion has been to her the "renouncer," who gives up everything for the sake of Truth, and goes forth with nothing but the yellow robe and the begging-bowl of the religious mendicant. These Westerners seem to her axiomatically irreligious just because they live so comfortably. But Sadhu Sundar Singh showed that Bhakti in an Indian Christian, just as in a Hindu ascetic, may mean giving up all things for Truth's sake. All over the country there have been large numbers of young Christians who have been stimulated to follow his example of re-

* See C. F. Andrews, *Sadhu Sundar Singh;* and Streeter and Appaswamy, *The Sadhu.*

nunciation and of a wandering apostolate. Their Devotion to Christ may be a main factor in leading up to that new thing which is so greatly to be desired, the interpretation of Christ in terms which India can understand. But however this interpretation comes, it will have to take into account, and to build upon, the foundations already well and truly laid, in Indian Bhakti religion. Both Greek philosophy and Jewish Law were acclaimed by the early Christian Fathers as "schoolmasters to Christ." In India it will not be philosophy that is the schoolmaster, great and glorious as are the achievements of Indian philosophy, but the poetry of the Pathway of Devotion.

XX

PANDITA RAMABAI

PANDITA RAMABAI is a shining example of modern Indian Bhakti. Her father was a Brahmin from Western India, belonging to the splendid stock from which came the Right Hon. G. K. Gokhale, the famous Indian statesman, Mr. B. G. Tilak, the leader of the Nationalists during the early years of this century, Narayan Vaman Tilak, the inspired Christian poet, Professor Karve, the founder of the first Women's University in India, and many other leaders, writers, teachers and men of religion.

Anant Shastri Dongre was deeply learned in Sanskrit. He was a man of a profoundly religious spirit, going on pilgrimage constantly, to one or another of the holy places of India. He lived for years with his wife and two children in a lonely settlement in the heart of the Gangamula forest, where their nearest neighbours were the tigers. He was regarded as scandalously heretical by orthodox Hindus, because he believed in the education of women; but in a debate on the subject, which lasted two months, and took place at a well-known monastery, he routed all his opponents. He taught his wife and daughter the Sanskrit language, which is extraordinarily difficult to learn, and did so with such success that his daughter became able to converse in it fluently. In earlier life this famous Brahmin scholar had been courted by the great and powerful to such an extent that one Prince is said to have given him Rs. 25,000 and another Rs. 175,000; but he always held before himself the ideal of the Hindu wandering ascetic;

and he renounced all his wealth to become an itinerant teacher. Thus from the time that Pandita Ramabai was six and a half she had no home, but wandered from place to place with her father, mother, sister and brother, first attending and then herself giving readings in the scriptures, and receiving whatever might be given in food or money as reward. The family gave away to the poor all that they did not need themselves.

Thus the young girl was trained in the self-renouncing spirit of the famous poetess-princess of the Bhakti school, Mirabai, who wrote:—

God have I bought: the price He asked I paid:
  Some cry "Too great," while others jeer " 'Twas small";
I paid in full, weighed to the utmost grain,
  My love, my life, my self, my soul, my all.

In 1876 the young girl's father, mother and sister all died in a famine, within a few months of each other. Her father's dying words to Ramabai were, "Always make it your aim to serve God . . . He will guard you, and you must always serve Him." The great scholar was now so poor that his children had themselves to carry his body two miles to the place where, being a *sannyasi* (a renouncer), he was buried, not burnt.

In Pandita Ramabai's youth women were thought of amongst orthodox Hindus as in a sense lower than animals. They were regarded as inherently bad, as worse even than demons. A woman as a woman could never gain salvation. Her only hope was to be re-born as a man, and such re-birth could come only through abject husband-worship. Hence the nameless tyranny of the orthodox Hindu husband. By 1878, when she was aged twenty, the girl's mind became filled with revolt against this whole system of ideas. By this time she could repeat by heart 18,000 verses of the Hindu scriptures. She knew Sanskrit grammar well, and could converse and make poems, in Sanskrit. Soon afterwards she was welcomed at the Calcutta University Senate House by three Sanskrit professors, two of whom were Englishmen. They chanted her praise in Sanskrit verse, to which she replied extemporaneously in the same. She was then given the title of Saraswati (the goddess of learning) by an assembly of Sanskrit scholars, or *pandits*, and thus became known as *Pandita*. Before long the girl-scholar was famous all over India; and the hope began to stir that she might permanently affect the position of Indian womanhood; for she made a public pronouncement in Calcutta condemning the seclusion of women and the practice of child-marriage, and urging women to learn Sanskrit.

In 1880 another crushing blow befell her; for she lost her brother, her only surviving relative. Soon after, she did an extremely daring thing, in marrying his friend, who was a Sudra, a low-caste man. She thus broke all the rules of orthodoxy at one fell swoop, and was immediately thrust beyond the caste-pale. Nineteen months later her husband died of cholera, leaving her with a baby girl.

Among her husband's books the Pandita found a Bengali copy of the Gospel of St. Luke, which she eagerly read.

In 1882 she came, alone but for her baby girl, to Poona, the centre of the virile Maratha culture. There she was welcomed by the great social reformer, Mr. Justice Ranade, as an important asset in the cause of the education of womanhood, which he had closely at heart. She founded in Poona a club for Indian ladies, to deliver them from child-marriage, ignorance and other evils, and began going from city to city to found branches of this club. She discovered that 99 men of every 100 were opposed to female education and emancipation, and that the women themselves were "ignorant, unpatriotic, selfish, uncultivated." Indeed she said of them:

"They drag the men down into the dark abyss, where they dwell together, without hope."

About this time the Hunter Commission on Education went out to India. The Pandita made an eloquent appeal to it for women doctors. This appeal was read by Queen Victoria, and led to the foundation of the Dufferin Hospitals for women, and to an immense amount of magnificent work on behalf of the suffering women of India, whom owing to social prejudice it is a very difficult matter for men doctors to treat.

In 1882 a girl-widow of twelve was brought to the Pandita. Like thousands upon thousands of other Hindu widows she was supposed to be a demon and to have destroyed her husband. The Pandita welcomed her to her home, seeing a great need summed up in the pathetic figure. She began at once to plan a Widows' Home; but could get little help from Hindus; and so (once again breaking with all orthodoxy by crossing the "black water"), she went off to England to collect money. Here she settled down with the Wantage Sisters, and a little later was baptized a Christian as a result of observing the girls' rescue work carried on by the Sisters. In 1883 she began teaching Sanskrit at Cheltenham Ladies' College, under the redoubtable Miss Beale. Indomitable as she was in character, the Pandita was diminutive in size, slight and weakly-looking; and during most of her life she was almost stone-deaf. These heavy handicaps must be kept in mind as we seek to appraise her work.

In 1886 she went to America, where she published her terrible book, *The High Caste Hindu Woman*, and studied kindergarten methods. In 1887 the Ramabai Association was founded in Boston, to give education to Indian child-widows. It helped her work greatly in the future. She travelled widely in the United States, lecturing; and in 1888 returned to India, having gained the support of thousands of sympathizers through her flaming redemptive zeal on behalf of Indian womanhood. Later she published an account of her travels which became a Marathi classic.

On reaching India once more she set to work immediately on her Widows' Home. In six months it had 25 pupils. The girls were left free to follow their own religion; but they were also free to attend the Pandita's family prayers, with the result that many began to want to become Christians, and a newspaper clamour broke out against her as a proselytizer, a clamour which continued off and on for the rest of her life.

The Pandita's first pupil had become a widow at the age of fifteen. Her jewels were stolen from her by her brother-in-law. Her head was shaved. She was only allowed the roughest garments. She was forced to beg for work and food, or starve. No one would give her work, because as a widow she was ill-omened. Filth instead of food was thrown into her begging-basket, since it was supposed that her husband had died because of her sins, perhaps committed in a previous life. She had to endure constant mockings and cruelty. Three times she had nearly committed suicide, but was restrained by the fear of re-birth as a widow. After four years at the Widows' Home this poor child re-married, became the mother of distinguished sons; and died after doing thirty years of splendid work for Indian womanhood. There were many such. In short, the Pandita's Widows' Home lit a fire which spread throughout India.

In 1891 Pandita Ramabai went through what she believed to be a conversion of the heart, her baptism eight years before having followed a merely intellectual convincement. Now, after a period of dark groping, she saw Christ on the Cross; and she spoke of her vision in the familiar terms of Indian Bhakti. She declared also that she could scarcely contain her joy.

In 1895, twelve girls from her Widows' Home were baptized as Christians. Thereupon twenty others were withdrawn in protest; but fresh applicants for admission kept coming from all over India; for the Pandita used to disguise herself as a religious mendicant, and to go from town to town seeking out special cases of cruelty and need. About this time she began to write Marathi religious lyrics. They were largely on the subject of the Cross of Christ, and yet were full of joy. Once more her fame and her sphere of activity had spread to the whole of India.

Then came the critical years in this great life. In 1897 there took place a frightful famine. Remembering her own child-hood experiences, and the loss of her relatives, the Pandita went to help, in the Central Provinces, where the need was greatest. Almost as soon as she reached the area where she was going to work, the Pandita was confronted with "three fam-ished, shelterless girls, clothed in dripping rags, suffering intense pangs of hunger along with the bitter cold of the wind, enduring a living death." A wholesale traffic in girls had sprung up, and roused all the fighting-instinct in the Pandita, who wrote, "The Lord has put it into my heart to save three hundred girls out of the famine districts, and I shall go to work in His name. . . . God is not known: He is not under-stood: He is *used*."

The question of finance did not trouble her, for she had complete confidence that the needful money would come in. And it did come in. Although she now had three hundred girls to provide for, they never lacked.

When plague came, the Pandita moved her large family away from Poona, where she had at first stationed them, to a place in the country, thirty miles south, where she established her famous settlement, called *Mukti* (Release). This move was in no sense a retirement from the world, for she had end-less visitors, to whom she showed bountiful hospitality.

Before leaving Poona she scathingly and publicly con-demned the Hindu social system, at a public meeting which attracted great attention. In face of threats of violence, which she fearlessly defied, she said to her opponents, "You may be slaves, but I am free." Then she turned to give the rest of her life to her oppressed sisters at Mukti.

In the great famine of 1900, which probably cost twenty million lives, numbers of the Pandita's helpers at Mukti, including eight of those rescued in the previous famine three years before, set out and gathered fresh famine-victims. The support of Mukti became a continuous miracle. The Pandita gave everything she had to the cause, and declared about this time, "I am literally penniless, with no income of any kind. I own nothing on earth, except a few clothes and my Bible." Yet by the end of 1900 she had nearly two thousand girls depending upon her for everything, food, shelter, education, moral training. Moreover most of them had come from deplorable conditions, and a large percentage were of low castes.

To deal with this immense and at times difficult community, the Pandita had 150 helpers, a school of 50 classes, a kindergarten with 400 children, a printing-press, weaving, industries, and much agriculture. She was up before four every morning, so hard did she work, but she was always serene, unhurried and courageous. She ran her estate of 100 acres, and her army of girls, like a general conducting a campaign. She had all manner of extraordinary difficulties to face, for instance the general atmosphere of fear which is bred by an effective belief in evil spirits. But she was a staunch believer in prayer, and on blank pages in her Bible are many hundreds of names of girls for whom she habitually prayed. In 1901 no less than 1,200 of them became Christians. She had a prayer-circle of 70, praying on behalf of the outside world; and she habitually sent bands of girls to witness to God's Truth in near-by places. One of her Western helpers said of her, "She radiated power."

The Pandita was a strong patriot; but she believed that

India could only become free as the bonds of social oppression were broken. She recommended revolutionary action to this end, i.e., a total break with Hinduism, as against the evolutionary methods advocated by other reformers. One of her favourite slogans was, "Proclaim liberty throughout all the land, and to all the inhabitants thereof." It is probable that her example did more than any other individual's to awaken the Hindu conscience to the evil position of Indian womanhood. The effects are seen all over India to-day, for example in the extremely important part women are playing in the modern national movement.

The Pandita's spirit is well summed up in her great saying, "Depending absolutely on our Father God, we have nothing to fear from anybody, nothing to lose, nothing to regret." A great poetess has called her "the first Christian to be enrolled in the calendar of Hindu saints." She showed conclusively what a genuinely Indian Bhakti of Jesus Christ can do for the cause of national regeneration.

XXI

MAULANA ABUL KALAM AZAD

THERE ARE NOW (1942) roughly one hundred millions of Moslems in India. Religiously they are divided into Shias and Sunnis, the latter being in a large majority. Politically they are divided, in what proportions no one can say, between the Pan-Islamist followers of the Moslem League, and the Nationalist followers of Maulana Abul Kalam Azad, the President of the Indian National Congress. The Moslem League stands for Pakistan, a word meaning "Holy Land," but said by the followers of the League to be composed as follows:—P for Punjab, A for Afghanistan (with the North-West Frontier Province), K for Kashmire, and ISTAN for the concluding letters of Baluchistan. This derivation is interesting for two reasons: in the first place it shows the extra-territorial significance of the Pakistan idea, since Afghanistan is included; in the second place it shows how expansive the idea is; for within three years of the launching of the Pakistan project the ambitions of its advocates had so increased as to make them include in their purview other regions with a Moslem majority in the population, Sind and Bengal.

Later, Haiderabad was also added, because it is under a Moslem ruler, though its population is predominantly Hindu. Meanwhile it was becoming increasingly obvious that westward the League looked towards other Islamic States in addition to Afghanistan.

All this means that Pakistan is a revival of the idea of a great Pan-Islamic Federation, or Federal Empire, an idea which has hovered for generations in the background of the thinking of many Indian Moslems. In such a Federal Empire the centre of population, wealth and power would inevitably fall in Moslem India; and Moslem India being scattered over the face of Hindu India, there could be no other possibility but that Hindu India should become a region subject to the imperial control of the Moslem Federal Empire.

These ideas have a strange fascination for many Britishers in India, even for some highly-placed officials. For generations there has been a feeling that the Moslem is "a bit of a sahib," somewhat like ourselves, or more like ourselves than the Hindu. His fighting qualities are admired. His religion is respected as in some ways remarkably akin to "Old Testament Christianity." If we have got to back out, it is felt that we had much better leave India to Moslem control than risk Congress rule.

On the other hand, to those who have learnt to love India as their foster-mother, and to understand something of the aspirations of her sons and daughters for her unity, freedom and nationhood, there can be nothing but despair in this Pakistan project. It would reduce India to less than a mere geographical expression. The advocates of Pakistan declare that the very word "India" is a mischievous lie. It would expose her to an imperialism for more intolerant and oppressive than our own—Islamic imperialism in the Near East has made deserts of lands once prosperous and highly civilized. It would very probably subject her to an ignorant and fanatical tyranny.

As we have seen, Pakistan lay in the essence of the Cripps proposals. "His Majesty's Government undertake to accept and implement forthwith the Constitution so framed subject only to: (1) the right of any Province of British India that is not prepared to accept the new Constitution to retain its present constitutional position, provision being made for its subsequent accession if it so decides. With such non-acceding

Provinces, should they so desire, His Majesty's Government will be prepared to agree upon a new Constitution, giving them the same full status as the Indian Union, and arrived at by a procedure analogous to that herein laid down."

In his broadcast to India explaining the proposals he had brought, delivered on March 30th, 1942, Sir Stafford Cripps said:—"Well, that's what we say to the Provinces of India. Come together to frame a common constitution. If you find after all your discussion and all the give-and-take of a constitution-making assembly that you cannot overcome your differences, and that some Provinces are still not satisfied with the constitution, then such Provinces can go out and remain out if they wish, and just the same degree of self-government and freedom will be available for them as for the Union itself —that is to say, complete self-government."

This means in effect Pakistan. And seeing that the proposals also look forward to the granting to the Indian States of the same right of non-accession to the Union, the (so far) final act of British imperialism in India is seen to be the offer of self-imposed vivisection. We are trying to cajole India to enter the war on our side by giving her the means of suicide and persuading her to use those means. It is *Divide et Impera* with a vengeance. If India is to tear herself in pieces like this (for Pakistan would mean civil war in six months), will not the British power be inevitably compelled to march in again to restore tranquility and order?

But there are other Moslems in India besides the adherents of Pakistan and the Moslem League. They are Nationalists, who recognize that the vast majority of Indian Moslems are of Indian race, and that their religion is no reason for their desiring to tear their motherland asunder. The leader of these Moslem Nationalists, and at present the leader of all Nationalist India, is Maulana Abul Kalam Azad.

His grandfather was the last great scholar to be given the title of "Pillar of Learning" by a Moghal Emperor. Long before that his distant ancestors had maintained a position of dignity and independence under difficult circumstances in the time of the Emperors Akbar and Jahangir. His father was a famous Sufi (Mohammedan mystic), and wrote many books in Arabic and Persian. He became a refugee from Delhi at the time of the sack of that city by the British in 1857. He eventually settled at Mecca, and his mind turned in horror from all things Western as a result of the experience he had been through. His son, Abul Kalam Azad, was born at Mecca in 1887, and grew up to use Arabic as his mother-tongue. He came to Calcutta for education in 1898, and accomplished the feat of passing through the extremely exacting Islamic course in Arabic and Persian, which is supposed to take fourteen years, in only four years. Later he studied at the famous Al Azhar University at Cairo. During the lifetime of his father the latter's conservatism prevented him from learning English; but he rapidly picked it up after his father's death, which occurred in 1909. He had already become a brilliant writer, and from the age of fourteen had been the editor of an Arabic periodical, and had been accustomed to lecturing on Islamic subjects.

The year 1909 was of great importance in the recent history of India, because it saw the introduction of the Minto-Morley Reforms of the principle of communal representation (i.e., the grouping of Moslems, Hindus and others in separate electorates and constituencies—a plan which results in a steady embitterment of the relations between the communities, since only fanatical party men have in practice a chance of election *). The responsibility for this disastrous step must largely

* Mahadev Desai in his *Life of Abul Kalam Azad* quotes Mr. Lionel Curtis as follows:—"The concession of communal representation is the greatest blunder ever committed by the British Government in India. So long as it remains, India will never attain to the unity of nationhood. The longer it remains the more difficult will it be to uproot it, till in the end it will only be eradicated at the cost of civil war. To enable India to attain nationhood is the trust laid on us, and in conceding the establishment of communal representation we have been false to that trust."

be laid at the doors of a Moslem Potentate, who led a deputation to Lord Minto to demand communal representation for his co-religionists. A letter from Morley to Minto shows, however, that this deputation was in a sense a "command performance"; for it says, "It was *your* early speech about their extra claims that first started the Muslim scare." At this stage Moslem Nationalism was almost non-existent; and the Mohammedans as a body were strenuously in support of the British system. One result of this attitude was their obtaining communal representation. However, though Abul Kalam Azad was still only a young man, he saw the danger of such tendencies, and in 1912 started a periodical, called *Al Hilal*, with the objective of turning his fellow-Moslems away from communalism towards Indian Nationalism.

Pan-Islamic tendencies were greatly strengthened by the Italo-Turkish war, by the Balkan wars, by the war of 1914–18, and by the long-continued agitation regarding the Khilafat (the position of the Sultan of Turkey as the supreme head of Islam) which accompanied the settlement between Turkey and the victorious Allies. Abul Kalam Azad saw more and more clearly the dangers of Pan-Islam; and his paper *Al Hilal*, which rapidly attained the (for India) large circulation of 25,000, and was written in the finely polished Urdu style, became more and more outspoken on the side of Indian Nationalism. Finally it was suspended by the Government, and its editor was interned at Ranchi from 1916 to 1920.

The Amritsar shootings of April, 1919, resulted in a huge swing of Indian Moslem opinion towards the Congress and Nationalism, a tendency which was increased by Mr. Gandhi's making the cause of the Khilafat his own during his non-cooperation movement of 1920–22. Abul Kalam Azad became immensely popular, and on his release from internment was asked to allow himself to be made by his co-religionists Imam (spiritual head of all Moslems) for the whole of India. He declined; but in 1923 he was elected President of the Indian National Congress, which position he holds again to-day (1942). In 1921 he spent a time in jail in connection with the boycott organized against the visit to India of the Prince of Wales.

It must be emphasised, as is done by my deceased friend Mahadev Desai, to whose invaluable little book on Abdul Kalam Azad I am greatly indebted, that this great Moslem leader is not merely a politician. He is also a man of letters, a great student incidentally of Byron, and a man of religion. In his statement to the court on his arrest in 1921, the following passage occurs:—

The iniquities of courts of law constitute an endless list and history has not yet finished singing the elegy of such miscarriages of justice. In that list we observe a holy personage like Jesus, who had to stand in his time before a foreign court and be convicted even as the worst of criminals. We see also in the same list Socrates, who was sentenced to be poisoned for no other crime than that of being the most truthful person of his age. We meet also the name of that great Florentine martyr to truth, the inventor Galileo, who refused to belie his observations and researches merely because their avowal was a crime in the eyes of constituted authority. . . . When I ponder on the great and significant history of the convict's dock and find that the honour of standing in that place belongs to me to-day, my soul becomes steeped in thankfulness and praise to God.

Later in the same statement the prisoner spoke thus of his religious faith:—

Islam constitutes a perfected system of freedom and democracy. It has been sent down to get back for the human race the liberty which has been snatched away from it. Monarchs, foreign dominations, selfish religious pontiffs, and powerful sections have alike misappropriated this liberty of man. They have fondly nursed the belief that power and possession spell the highest right. The moment Islam appeared, it proclaimed that the highest right is not might but right itself. No one except God has got the right to make serfs and slaves of God's creatures. All men are equal and their fundamental rights are on a par. He only is greater than others whose deeds are the most righteous of all."

In 1922 the Maulana took the lead in the movement for persuading Moslems to give up the sacrificing of cows, in deference to Hindu beliefs. In this and other ways he has worked hard for reconciliation between Hindus and Moslems, often at considerable risk to himself during times of critical tension between the two communities. He has also worked for reconciliation in other spheres. When in 1936–7, Congress ministries took over control of eight of the eleven British-Indian Provinces, and started a courageous enterprise of social reconstruction, his advice, arbitration and encouragement were always at hand to make settlements possible between conflicting groups, for example, land-owners and tenants.* Thus in Bihar it was largely through his influence that rents were reduced by 25 per cent. or more, and that the tenants secured rights which made them practically proprietors of their lands, subject only to the payment of rent, and which guaranteed them moreover from liability to be ejected for non-payment of rent. His arbitration was invaluable also in reconciling the conflicting claims of Government and land-lords, in Bihar, over the thorny question of the introduction of the Income Tax in agricultural areas.

Then came the declaration by the Viceroy, in September, 1939, that India was at war with Germany—a declaration made without consulting Indian opinion, and a declaration which was felt to demonstrate that "India was still a dependency." At the same time the Pakistan project for the vivisecting of India came to the fore, to receive official blessings in the Cripps Proposals of 1942. Nationalist India felt as we

* The Maulana proves conclusively in his writings that there was no oppression of Moslem or other minorities under these Congress ministries.

should feel if a foreign imperialist government proposed that the English counties whose names end in -sex (and in which we must suppose that a majority of the population have retained an active sympathy with their Saxon cousins in Germany) should be entirely detached from English nationhood, with the prospect of their throwing in their lot with Germany! The Maulana has been outspoken in his expression of his views on such a situation, and in his advocacy of drastic measures for meeting it. In consequence he is now, with the other Congress leaders, in jail.

But we shall never solve our problems in India by jailing India's leaders. It is well that we should remind ourselves that Mr. Gandhi has declared that he would prefer Moslem to British rule; and that he feels that the issues involved in the present situation are nothing less than India's loyalty to or rejection of her age-old principles of non-violence.

We may conclude this chapter with one or two more quotations from the Maulana's writings. First on the place of Islam in India:—

Islam has now as great a claim on the soil of India as Hinduism. If Hinduism has been the religion of the people here for several thousands of years, Islam has also been their religion for a thousand years. Just as a Hindu can say with pride that he is an Indian and follows Hinduism, so also we can say with equal pride that we are Indians and follow Islam. I shall enlarge this orbit still further. The Indian Christian is equally entitled to say with pride that he is an Indian and is following a religion of India, namely Christianity.

He speaks thus for reconciliation between India and England, and they are words worth weighing:—

Is it impossible that two great peoples of the world, who have been tied together by the course of events as rulers and ruled, should create a new relationship between them, based on reason, justice and peace . . . If the British people could have proudly said to the world to-day that they had added a new example to history, what a vast and unparalleled triumph this would have been for humanity! Certainly this is not an impossibility; but it is an amazingly difficult thing to do."

This on his religious faith:—

There are language, race, colour and countless other divisions— rich and poor, master and servant, high-born and low-born, strong and weak, and so on. All these divisions cannot but make for discord and strife. What then is the silken string that can thread these scattered beads and make of divided mankind one united brotherhood? That silken string, that sacred link, is the Worship of One God. How much-so-ever divided you may be, you cannot have different Gods. You are the servants of One Lord, and your prayers and worship are before the One Sacred Throne. No matter what your race, tribe or country, the moment you surrender yourselves to one Father, He will put an end to all your quarrels and unite your hearts together. You will then realize that the world is your country and mankind is one family, and you are children of the same Father."

XXII

M. K. GANDHI

IN HIS YOUTH, M. K. Gandhi, who has become so portentous a challenge to our whole Western civilization, was apparently quite an ordinary young man. During his career as a law-student in London, and for years afterwards in South Africa, he was immaculately dressed in the latest fashion of men's wear; and was well launched, it seemed, upon a convention-ally prosperous career. Then as he himself tells us in his *Story of My Experiments with Truth*, everything became changed for him by the study of four great books, which we also must study if we are to comprehend the man and his message. These books are, Ruskin's *Unto This Last*, Tolstoy's *The Kingdom of God is Within You*, the *Bhagavad Gita*, and the *New Testament*.

As a result of his study of these books, Mr. Gandhi has developed a clearly-marked idealism, which he has had the genius to make the guiding force behind a vast movement of world-recovery. In this movement the best elements in the spiritual heritage both of East and West are combined.

At the very base of his idealism is belief in God. "I am a man of faith," he says, "my reliance is wholly on God" (*Harijan*, 20th October, 1940). "I am surer of God's existence than of the fact that you and I are sitting in this room. I can also testify that I may live without air and water, but not without Him" (*Harijan*, 14th May, 1938). He insists that it is only as this vital and fundamental faith in God is shared by a whole people that it can achieve its true destiny: "No power on earth can stop the march of a peaceful, determined and God-fearing people."

From this God-centred outlook on the world comes a spirit of self-identification with the sufferings of needy humanity. The poverty of India is such that according to one distinguished authority, the great mass of the population go to bed not only hungry, but ravenous, almost every night of their lives. Another authority has declared that in especially poor districts with which he is familiar, it is the lot of thousands to consider themselves lucky if they get a wretched meal every other day. To Mr. Gandhi these things are not mere dry economic facts. They are a battle-cry, demanding action; and the first action which they demand is that of the patriot's identifying himself with these sufferers. Once he was invited to visit a leper colony in Orissa. He came and addressed the lepers; and then, when he had finished speaking, he said to himself, "Why should I call these people my brothers, if I do not mix with them?" He then insisted that each of the stricken creatures should be brought before him, and paying no heed to their loathsome condition, he shook each of them by the hand, caressed them, and spoke words of comfort to them. "I claim to be born a democrat," he has said: "if complete identification with the poorest of mankind, longing to live no better than they, and corresponding conscious effort to approach that level to the best of one's ability, can entitle one to make that claim."

At any meeting arranged for him, if a special enclosure is set apart for the poorest and lowest of the Outcastes, Gandhi will go and take his own place in that enclosure. At his famous trial, in 1922, when asked to describe himself, he replied, "I am a peasant and a weaver." The immense hold which he has gained over the rank and file of the Indian population is largely to be accounted for by the fact that the people realize that he has made himself one with them in their deepest needs.

Closely connected with this self-identification with the common people is Gandhi's simplicity of life. A friend of mine has lately (1942) called upon him at his village home near Wardha in the Central Provinces. He found the great man in a tiny white-washed room in a small cottage, where he was forming polices and dictating statements which would affect the whole of India. Other visitors have noticed how accessible he is. Whilst he is at work, a constant stream of peasant admirers passes silently through the room behind him, each individual pausing for a moment to gain that vision of a great spiritual teacher which in India is traditionally regarded as a guarantee of a better lot in the next "birth." He is a man also of great austerity of life. On his march to the coast, to break the Government salt monopoly, in March, 1930, he insisted on walking fifteen miles a day on foot, and refused to use the horse and the bullock-carts brought for his service, though he permitted the weaker members of his suite to do so. In accordance with his usual habit, he set the example (and insisted on his suite's following it), of spinning three hours a day, it being a fundamental belief with him that action must accompany words. "Thirty-four years of continuous experience and experimenting in truth and non-violence have convinced me that non-violence cannot be sustained unless it is linked to conscious body-labour and finds expression in our daily contact with our neighbours. This is the constructive programme. . . . My experiments in non-violence have taught me that non-violence in practice means common labour with the body" (*Harijan*, 27th January, 1940). His hand-spinning is therefore not only a programme for the revival of cottage-industries and the combating of peasant unemployment. It is much more than this. It is a sharing of the lot of the peasant labourers, a sacrament of self-identification with them, and a means of self-discipline in preparation for wielding the great weapon of non-violent resistance to evil.

With hand-spinning Gandhi connects four other causes, opposition to drunkenness, unity between Hindus and Moslems, the abolition of Untouchability, and the raising of the position of women, especially in regard to child-marriage. These are the "five fingers" of the hand with which he strikes for social reform.

He has a profound belief in the powers of leadership possessed by Indian womanhood. From time to time he has sent his own wife as an ambassador to settle vexed questions, as in the case of the complaints of mis-government in Rajkot State in 1939. An English visitor to India in 1930 wrote home, "The women are on the march: they are everywhere breaking from the shackles of purdah and caste-tyranny; Mahatma Gandhi has given them the signal, by setting their services in the forefront of the national movement: everywhere one may feel around one in this country the bursting forth of new life." The development of women's leadership since 1930 has been rapid and continuous. During the "troubles" in the earlier years of the period, there were in many parts of India women "dictators" carrying forward, often with the greatest courage, the work of the Congress whilst their men-folk were in jail. Later on, women began to come into their own in the years of Congress Government in the eight provinces between 1936 and 1939. The amazing progress that has been made is very largely due to Mr. Gandhi.

Closely allied also with his simplicity is this great man's humility. He once declared, in estimating the comparative value, as it were, of certain virtues, that he himself put humility above love, because love might be interpreted as meaning an unwarrantable interference with a second personality. On another occasion, in speaking to an English visitor, he said, "I am just an ordinary human being, and full of weaknesses and sins. But I have this one thing that the poor recognize in me at once. They know that I share all their hardships. You could have the same influence if you would do the same."

This element in Gandhi's character was brought very prominently before the public eye in 1932, when he was in prison, and underwent a fast expressly on behalf of the Untouchables, who (he felt) were not getting a fair deal either from the Government or from their fellow-countrymen in connection with the discussions then going forward about the new federal constitution. This fast, though it only lasted about a week, brought Mr. Gandhi to the edge of the grave. The various communities affected got together in frenzied haste, composed their differences, and agreed to grant the Untouchables a very generous measure of representation in the proposed new legislatures, on terms which Mr. Gandhi felt he could accept, i.e., without the odious and extremely perilous device of communal representation, which (he believed) would brand them as Untouchables for evermore, and would wound India even more grievously than the Hindu-Moslem division had done. The Prime Minister of England himself took part in bringing about action of unprecedented speed on this issue. The proposed alternatives to communal representation were examined and approved, just in time to save Mr. Gandhi's life. In this crucial instance it was realized how the great man made himself one with the humblest of his fellow-countrymen, with a creative self-renunciation which welcomed them into the Indian body-politic even at the cost of his own suffering and at the risk of his own life. His action had demonstrated a method by which cantankerous disputes, which have lasted for many centuries, may be rapidly composed, immemorial wrongs boldly placarded, and the machinery for their righting set vigorously in motion. He had shown even how the mills of distant imperial control may be set grinding with unprecedented speed.

On Mr. Gandhi's recovery and release came a great campaign for the liberation of the Untouchables all over India. He toured the country, identifying himself as much as possible with the Untouchables wherever he went, and urging

that their ancient wrongs should be righted. As the campaign
went forward, he felt that he could no longer ride about in a
motor-car, descending from it at infrequent intervals like a
being from another world, for a few minutes of benignant
advice. He must go farther than this in self-identification with
those whom he would serve. And so the campaign closed with
the old man walking on foot from village to village (and those
who went with him said that he did it at a remarkable pace).
The newspaper reports of his journeys changed from the
order of so many hundred miles a week and so many tens of
thousands of rupees collected for the liberation-campaign, to
the order of sixty or seventy miles walked and a few hundreds
of rupees collected. But the distances covered and the amounts
collected did not really matter. India realized that in the burning and blistering hot-weather, when the slightest activity is
an insupportable burden and the peasant waits limply at
home for the rains to break, her great saint and prophet was
marching steadily forward on foot from village to village, for
the sake of his disinherited and despised fellow-countrymen,
with whom he had humbly made himself one. In consequence
the campaign of liberation all over the country went ahead
with increased zeal and success.

Many years ago, Mr. Gandhi realized that the effort to
identify himself with the world's suffering must lead him
beyond personal acquisitiveness and possessiveness. He told
me in 1931 how, when quite a young man, he had decided, on
one memorable night in South Africa, that he would never
again call anything his own. "I have kept to that resolve," he
continued, "and now although I am a man with immeasurable
resources at my command, I possess absolutely nothing. From
that decision, so long ago, there came into my life joy, freedom and power; and if you would know these things, you also
must tread the same path." The decision worked itself out in
the discovery of a new way of life, without personal property,

but in community, like the life lived in the ancient Indian
forest-settlements of teachers and pupils. He urged that we
in this country should attempt the same solution for the problem of unemployment, which at that time was assuming
gigantic proportions. He believed, he said, in the founding of
land-settlements, in which ex-members of the possessing class
should co-operate with unemployed families in a communal
way of life beyond personal possessions; and he told me how
three times over, in three different countries, the Transvaal,
Natal, and Gujerat, he had founded and lived in such land-
settlements.

But it is time to return to the real springs of Mr. Gandhi's
power and influence, his spiritual life. We were told, in 1931,
that there are three sayings of the New Testament, above
all others, by which he guides his practice and behaviour:—
"Take no thought for the morrow"; "Be careful for nothing"; "Sufficient unto the day is the evil thereof." The
tremendous strain put upon him by entire accessibility, by
constant living in public, and by the necessity for continuous
negotiating with representatives of divergent and often hostile
interests, can only be overcome as he lives in the spirit of
detachment and of complete dependence upon God, as that
spirit is expressed in those three sayings. For many years he
has found that he can only dwell rightly in that spirit as he
sets aside one day in each week for complete silence; and also
as he makes it a practice to rise very early each morning for
the sake of prayer and meditation. "Humble and constant
endeavour and silent prayer are always my two trusty com-
panions along the weary but beautiful path that all seekers
must tread." There is a constant emphasis in his writings on
this essential matter of private prayer; and it is here that he
realizes, as he has put it, that "There is nothing permanent,
nothing everlasting, save God Himself."

This life-discipline has also been expressed by Mr. Gandhi

as follows:—"Worship and prayer are no superstition; they are acts more real than the acts of eating, drinking, sitting, walking. It is no exaggeration to say that they alone are real, all else is unreal."

At the trial of 1922, Mr. Gandhi's English judge himself called him "a man of high ideals and of noble and even saintly life." His chief claim to such a character is the heart-felt aspiration which he has himself worded thus: "It is my frequent prayer to God that I may lay down my life in the service of the poor. . . . To see the all-pervading Spirit of Truth face to face, one must be able to love the meanest of creatures as oneself."

XXIII

SATYAGRAHA

WE HAVE CONSIDERED various aspects of the personality of Mr. Gandhi. We must now turn to the distinctive method of political and social action which he has discovered and revived, through his study of the four great documents of faith which have been named, and (as he would himself say) through the working of the guidance of God in his spirit.

Years ago he used to call this method of action Ahimsa, which may be translated Harmlessness or Non-Violence; but of recent years, feeling this term too negative, he has chosen a new one, Satyagraha, Defence of Truth. He has employed this method of action (for such it is) both in South Africa and in India, using it to prevent war, to put an end to social injustice, to combat invidious legislation, to obtain political rights, to end industrial strife, and for a variety of other purposes.

The history of Satyagraha goes back to Gautama the Buddha, and beyond. Its essence is that it springs out of a character and a spirit such as we have been studying in Mr. Gandhi—a character and a spirit, that is, marked by simplicity, humility, faith in the unseen forces of the Spirit, and above all, by self-identifying, loving and redemptive compassion for the poor, the needy and the suffering.

Satyagraha is put into practice when men of this type of character and spirit—or one such man only—consciously and deliberately take upon themselves a sharing of pain to end pain, as Gautama did when he left his royal palace and became a penniless seeker after truth in order that he might find the secret of the conquest of the world's suffering.

The Christian consciousness can best understand the meaning of Satyagraha if it is called "the method of the Cross"; and indeed Mr. Gandhi himself was directly inspired by the New Testament in the most notable of his Satyagraha enterprises, that embodied in the fast of 1924 for the ending of war between Hindus and Moslems. He would himself be the first to acknowledge that in seeking thus to follow Christ in the method of the Cross mistakes and failures have crept in, and lack of purity of motive, i.e., lack of complete selflessness, has again and again hindered success. But at the same time, Satyagraha embodies the largest-scale and most noteworthy of all modern attempts to make the Cross rule in human affairs.

There are four main elements in the idealism of Satyagraha. In the first place, there is the realization that evil exists. We are not to live in a fool's paradise, but are to acquaint ourselves at first hand with the actual facts of class-oppression, industrial exploitation, imperial dominance, as these facts spell themselves out in terms of human poverty, misery and pain. We have got to understand all this not merely in abstract intellectual comprehension, but with the sympathetic imagination which sees the human values involved. It is an affair both of mind and of feeling.

In the second place, there must be the resolve at all costs to end the suffering. This is a question of the stimulation of the will. Many people know that pain and wrong exist, but privilege and security prevent their doing anything about it, and keep them apathetic. Satyagraha demands action against wrong and against the pain that is caused by wrong.

In the third place, Satyagraha realizes that wrong and man-made pain can never be ended by violence. Forcibly to repress evil merely drives it underground, whence it is bound to

appear later with redoubled virulence, as the Nazi mentality
developed after Versailles. God did not even prevent the
supreme crime of the crucifixion of Christ by violence. No
thunderbolt struck down the Roman soldiers who drove home
the nails. Even if the sinner is utterly destroyed by violence,
since the sin is an evidence of evil will, it will reappear in other
men's evil will.

In the fourth place, Satyagraha teaches that, although
wrong and man-made pain cannot be ended by violence, they
can be ended by the redemptive good-will which is willing to
seek out ways of taking the suffering upon oneself, and sharing it to the utmost, even to death, without resentment or
recrimination towards the evil-doer, but patiently and lov-
ingly. Given this spirit in the Satyagrahi (he who practises
Satyagraha), the evil will which causes the wrong and the
suffering will be changed into good-will, with the result that
the wrong and suffering will be blotted out. The Satyagrahi
himself (or in our Western parlance, the Cross-bearer) may
never see this result; for it may well be that the evil will was
strong enough to kill him; but in this case a spiritual resurrec-
tion is absolutely certain; for through his self-sacrificing death
the good-will—the spirit of mercy, fellowship and love—will
triumph.

Satyagraha, it is also to be noticed, acts by means of appeal-
ing to the best element in the individual or the group which
is embodying the evil will and so imposing suffering and
oppression upon others. It never ceases to believe that this
element is there in the oppressors, however heartless they
may seem. It takes all risks, and is absolutely undefeatable in
its optimism in making its appeal, which it does by going into
the heart of the suffering and wrong and bearing its share un-
complainingly. Thus:—"It is Gandhi's fundamental belief
in the innate sense of justice in the British character as susceptible to generous feeling that carried him forward with a

certainty of moral victory. His whole theory of moral warfare depends upon a belief in the generous response of human
nature. This principle, when applied in action, he calls Satyagraha." *

This aspect of Mr. Gandhi's idealism was strikingly ex-
emplified in the fast of 1924. As soon as it began, the better
element in both Hindus and Moslems was immensely reinforced, with the result that friendship rapidly took the place
of hatred in the relationships of the two communities.

One or two further comments must be made on the "ideol-
ogy" of Satyagraha.

In the first place, Satyagraha cannot spring "out of the
blue." It has to be based on a character and spirit which is
permanently in sympathy with the world's need. In Mr.
Gandhi himself this character and spirit make him say, "I am
a thief if I possess anything of which my brother stands in
need."

In the second place, Satyagraha may be put into action uni-
laterally. "I hold that for the full play of non-violence only
one party need believe in it" (Mr. Gandhi, in *Harijan*, 7th
October, 1939). It flourishes on opposition. It can even be
exercised, as Mr. Gandhi himself has shown on various occasions, when there is only one man who believes in it, and
although he is opposed by the embattled might of governments, wealth, and vested interests.

In the third place, it is a method which can be used by
women. "If only women will forget that they belong to the
weaker sex, I have no doubt that they can do infinitely more
than men against war. . . . Woman, I hold, is the person-
ification of self-sacrifice; but unfortunately to-day she does
not realize what a tremendous advantage she has over man.
. . . The Indian women played a more effective part in our
last non-violent war than men. The reason is simple. Non-

* C. F. Andrews, in the *International Review of Missions*, April, 1934.

violent war calls into play suffering to the largest extent, and
who can suffer more purely and nobly than women? . . .
The matchless beauty of Satyagraha lies in the fact that
though it is the weapon of the strongest, it can be wielded
by the weak in body, by the aged and even by children, if
they have stout hearts. And since resistance in Satyagraha is
offered through self-suffering, it is a weapon pre-eminently
open to women." (Mr. Gandhi, in *Young India*, 14th January, 1932.)

In the fourth place, the Satyagrahi must train himself "in
feeding the starving and clothing the naked and generally
serving the masses in this time of their need" (*Harijan*, 8th
February, 1942). Details are given in recent issues of *Harijan*
of the fashion in which the present war is embittering the
lot of the poor in various parts of India (for example, in certain areas of the Bombay Presidency peasants are being compelled to do forced labour for the landlords with a remunera-
tion of one penny a day); and suggestions are made for
Satyagrahis to undertake the organization of collective farms,
through which cooperative methods would be employed to
lighten the sufferings of the poor. This is evidence of the fact
that preparation for Satyagraha is not merely an affair of
intellectual enlightenment regarding the facts of poverty, nor
is it merely an affair of sympathy and fellow-feeling. It is
self-training through arduous and practical action, especially
in cooperative agriculture.

The technique by which Satyagraha operates (if the phrase
may be permitted) was worked out on a broad stage, and
under conditions of the greatest interest and importance, by
Mr. Gandhi himself during his career in South Africa. The
history of that epoch may be read in his own *Story of My
Experiments with Truth*, or in C. F. Andrews' *Mahatma
Gandhi's Ideas*. It may be summed up by saying that when
Mr. Gandhi returned to India in 1915, he had strong reason

for believing that he brought with him, originally learnt from the New Testament, the *Gita*, Ruskin and Tolstoy, and perfected by a long process of trial and error in South Africa, a new-old political and social weapon, which rightly employed would break any tyranny, whether of caste, class or government. The employment of this weapon demands the spreading of a spirit of active good-will and the embodiment in the Satyagrahi of a practical ideal of character. This is to be achieved first by prophetic utterance and fearless witnessing regarding the existence of great wrongs and man-made sufferings; then by a call to endure death rather than allow the continuance of the wrong and suffering; then by a leading-forth of those who have been brought to realize that, whilst violence can achieve nothing, patiently endured sharing of suffering cannot fail in the long run to change the evil will into good-will. They must court imprisonment or death till the wrong be righted, but always in the spirit of good-will, towards oppressors as well as oppressed. The South African government had given way before this formidable weapon, as used by the Indian coal-miners of Newcastle, in Natal, against invidious anti-Indian legislation. The time would surely come when the same weapon would be used in India.

As soon as he reached India, Mr. Gandhi realized that the outstanding wrong afflicting his home-land was man-made poverty, which kept the vast mass of his fellow-countrymen in abysmal suffering. We can only rightly understand the subsequent history of Satyagraha and of Mr. Gandhi himself as we recognize this fact. The political significance of his action has always been strictly subordinate to the social. He believes that *Indian poverty is caused poverty;* and that the cause of it is an iniquitous economic system maintained by the essential facts of imperialist control. He attacks British imperialism, by means of Satyagraha, and he attacks the landlord system, and he attacks Untouchability, because they bring about and perpetuate poverty.

The early Satyagraha compaigns in India, i.e., those between 1915 and 1919, were indeed almost entirely connected with economic questions. They were aimed at abolishing the system of indenture, at improving the condition of plantation-workers, at obtaining fairer conditions for mill-hands, and at lightening rents.

Then, in 1919, came the first attempt to extend the action of Satyagraha into the political sphere in a campaign against imperialism. This was in the Non-cooperation Movement of 1919–22. But the people as a whole were not sufficiently prepared, and violence broke out, followed by Mr. Gandhi's arrest. After his release in 1924 came the very notable use of Satyagraha against the war-fever between Hindus and Moslems, and in defence of the Untouchables at Vaikom in the South. From time to time since that period all manner of social and industrial issues have been tackled by Satyagraha; and a long series of political campaigns has been undertaken, the net result of which may be summed up on the one hand in the wounding and imprisoning by the police of tens of thousands of Satyagrahis, and on the other in the wide measure of provincial self-government enjoyed under the Congress Ministries of 1936. Satyagraha may work with extraordinary speed, or it may work slowly. By now (1942), the deepest foundations of imperialism have quite obviously been fatally shaken; but there is no saying yet when the new free and united India, for which Mr. Gandhi looks and on whose behalf he suffers, will come to be built.

The spirit in which he regards this political aspect of the use of Satyagraha may be summed up in words written by Mr. Gandhi many years ago:—"We must love our English administrators, and pray to God that they may have wisdom to see what appears to us to be their error. I believe in the power of suffering to melt the stoniest heart. We must by our conduct demonstrate to every Englishman that he is as safe in the remotest corner of India as he professes to feel behind his machine-gun. Either we believe in God and His righteousness, or we do not." The British system is buttressed on Indian poverty; and battens upon Indian poverty. Therefore, it must go. It must be ended not by violence but by willingness to share the poverty and to challenge the power which causes that poverty, in ways that have involved torture and loss of liberty for tens of thousands of Indians without shedding the blood of a single Englishman. C. F. Andrews once watched a crowd of Satyagrahis approaching a line of police, in the course of a disciplined protest against a wrong and oppressive use of its power by the Government. He saw the police *lathis* go up, and a long line of Satyagrahis fall senseless to the ground, with skulls battered and shoulders and collar-bones broken. Immediately another rank stepped quietly forward to take their place, and to suffer a similar fate. C. F. Andrews said it was the most terrible, and yet in a sense the most glorious thing he had ever seen.

Finally, Mr. Gandhi has written: "It was the New Testament which really awakened me to the value of Passive Resistance. When I read in the Sermon on the Mount such passages as 'Resist not him that is evil.' . . . 'He that smiteth thee on the right cheek, turn to him the other also.' . . . and 'Love your enemies, pray for them that persecute you, that ye may be the sons of your Father which is in heaven,' I was overjoyed. . . . The *Gita* deepened the impression, and Tolstoy's *Kingdom of God is Within You* gave it a permanent form."

Thus it was that Mr. Gandhi once opened a University Commemoration Day with an Inaugural Speech consisting of reading the Sermon on the Mount and adding the words, "This is what we need for India."

XXIV

JAWAHIRLAL NEHRU

In many ways, Nehru is the antithesis of Gandhi. He was educated at Harrow and Trinity College, Cambridge; and is deeply Westernized in his outlook. He has very little use for religion, which he is inclined to regard as "the opium of the people." He is a convinced Socialist, of a type of mind which would approve of physical force (one feels) were not his great leader's influence so strongly set against all violence. He is actively interested in Russia, and not in the spiritual and prophetic Russia represented by Tolstoy, but in the severely practical Russia of the Communist Party.

Nehru is a national leader of first-class quality, with an unlimited capacity for suffering in the cause of his ideals. He has endured eight terms of imprisonment, several of them under very rigorous conditions. He is a man of great personal magnetism; and his appeal to the young is irresistible. He is also a writer of great skill and force, as is evidenced by his *Autobiography*, by his *Glimpses of World History* and by other work. The story of his pilgrimage towards Socialism is excellently recorded in the *Autobiography*. He tells how Nationalism by itself gradually began to appear to him a narrow and insufficient principle, and how he began to perceive that freedom for individual, for community and for State depends on the uprooting of subversive profit-hunting selfishness, and on the launching of collectivist institutions. He demands the ending of imperialism for this object, because he sees that Socialism can never come into being so long as imperialism is there to bolster up a parasitic class of landlords and capitalists, without whose support imperialism could not exist. National freedom he sees less and less as an end in itself, and more and more as a means to social emancipation on the one hand and affiliation to a union of socialist states on the other.

He unites with Gandhi and with the ancient Indian tradition on one most important point, the condemnation of the profit-motive. The establishment of a socialist order, both within India herself and in a federation of similarly-constituted nations, depends, he believes, upon the effective elimination of this motive. Two thousand years ago the *Gita* taught this truth—that happiness and well-being for individual and community can only be attained as men cease to "desire the fruits of action," and learn to perform their function in life in the spirit of service to God and to the community. The whole history of Europe since the break-down of the mediaeval equilibrium (in which this bidding of the *Gita* was unconsciously in large measure fulfilled), proves that the *Gita* is right; and that Jesus Christ was right when He said, "Ye cannot serve both God and Mammon," and "Seek not for yourselves treasure on earth," and when He told the story of the Rich Fool. Nehru has come to believe that the profit-motive can, and must, be helped out of the track of human advance, by wise government action. Yet he does not belong to the apocalyptic type of Socialism, which holds that nothing can be effective to this end but a clean sweep (violent, if need be) and a fresh beginning. He welcomes, on the other hand, such small mercies as the gradual conversion of the National Congress to a belief in State-ownership of essential services, and State-abolition of outstanding wrongs by piecemeal action.

None the less he looks to a vastly increased tempo of change at no distant date, particularly when at last the grip of imperialism is loosened, and India becomes genuinely independent.

We have studied various aspects of that synthesis of East
and West which is coming about in modern India. In the
sphere of religion we have seen how the Bhakti-tradition
linked with Christianity may lead both India to a fresh understanding of the Pathway of Devotion, and the West to a fresh
understanding of Jesus Christ. Such men as Narayan Vaman
Tilak and Sandhu Sundar Singh, and such a woman as Pandita
Ramabai, show how rich may be the gain of mankind as a
whole, in literature, in spiritual attainment and in redemptive
social service, when once such a synthesis has been effected.

Mr. Gandhi in the second place shows us how the East may
re-interpret and re-apply the idealism of the Cross; and how
that idealism may so capture the imagination and inspire the
will of large masses of humanity that wars may be ended,
vested interests overthrown, ancient wrongs righted, and the
poor granted their just rights. Here again is a synthesis; and
the joint contribution of East and West may become of incalculable benefit to mankind as a whole.

Nehru is also for a synthesis, but on a different plane. He
too has come to understand the appalling poverty of his native
land, and the modern significance of her ancient teachings
regarding the extinction of the desire for personal profit and
advantage. He looks to the material and social organization
developed for the ending of poverty in the great Russian
experiment, to achieve the same purpose in India. But he is
more than half in sympathy also with the Russian conviction
that religion is a dangerous false-issue.

Nehru is severely critical of Gandhi's hand-spinning project
as a means of combating agricultural unemployment, and adding to agricultural earnings. He believes that the whole enterprise is too individualistic; and that it constitutes a harking-
back to the pre-industrial age. Gandhi, he believes, is inclined
to try to put the clock back, and to reject the benefits as well
as the disadvantages of Western culture. He (Nehru) wants

something much more radical and much more comprehensive than a mere tinkering with externals and fostering of cottage-industries. He believes that the whole agrarian system must be drastically overhauled. Especially in regard to the fragmentation of holdings, that system is collapsing before our eyes. As the population increases, and the holdings get smaller and smaller, they become progressively less workable, less productive, less able to support human life even on a standard of abject poverty. There is only one solution, the collective farm, with all land held and worked in common, except for cottage-gardens, and with big-scale husbandry thus rendered possible. The agricultural cooperative societies, now well over the hundred thousand in number, are showing the way; but the pace of advance must be greatly quickened, and that soon; for otherwise nation-wide and permanent famine is the only prospect ahead.

Over against rural unemployment, as he points out, there is a vast mass of urgently-needed work waiting to be done, especially in the construction of roads, the provision of irrigation schemes, the erection of better housing, the extension of sanitation and of medical facilities, electrification, and so forth. But he does not believe that these great tasks can be adequately tackled under existing institutions. He looks for a socialist India as only able to bridge the gap between idle labour and these urgent tasks.

Nehru acknowledges his own middle-class origin. His father was a wealthy land-owner, though at the same time a famous Nationalist. The son calls himself "one of the repentant bourgeoisie": and knows that he has still clinging round him many of the prejudices in the midst of which he was brought up. In spite of this he sees clearly that a drastic purging is needed not merely with regard to the imperial government, but also in the Indian class-situation. He hopes to bring about the change with as little suffering as possible; but the system will have to go, root and branch, and the individuals or groups that continue to cling to it will have to go too.

Nehru is especially outspoken with regard to the Indian States. Gandhi took a decisive step towards reform in this quarter when, in 1939, he undertook personal Satyagraha in order to set right a case of misgovernment in a State of Western India of which his own father had once been Prime Minister. On that occasion the Viceroy, the Home government, and the Congress Ministries in the eight provinces all cooperated in making his Satyagraha effectual; and in consequence a precedent was set which will certainly be of the highest importance for reform in the years ahead. For decade after decade, up to that time, though people of good-will knew how appalling were the conditions in many of the India States, nothing effective had been done for reform. But Gandhi's action set the ball rolling; and Nehru is much more radical in his attitude than Gandhi. He believes that the Indian States represent what is probably "the extremist type of autocracy existing in the world"; and he upbraids Gandhi for the politic slowness of the purging process which he advocates. He has no use, for instance, for Gandhi's belief that the Princes, or some of them, may come to fulfil a useful purpose in India if they will grant autonomy to their subjects, and rule over them as trustees. He quotes significantly a sinister utterance by one of the leading Princes, made in 1935 in the Chamber of Princes at Delhi:—"The Princes have no intention of allowing themselves to be destroyed by anybody, and should the time unfortunately come when the Crown is unable to afford the Indian States the necessary protection in fulfilment of its treaty obligations, the Princes and States will die fighting to the bitter end."

Nehru is emphatic also with regard to that major curse of the Indian countryside, the money-lender. Mr. H. N. Brailsford once wrote, "Indian usurers and landlords are the most rapacious parasites to be found in any contemporary social system." The two classes are now inextricably intermingled; often landlords in their artificially protected position (under the Permanent Settlement made by Lord Cornwallis in 1793, and similar arrangements) have become degenerate, and their lands have thus fallen into the hands of money-lenders, who have become landlords in their place. They too will in their turn become degenerate, but in the meantime what of the appalling misery inflicted upon the peasantry? In 1943 food-hoarding by this class is starving India.

Here also the remedy is collectivized agriculture. We are reminded in this connection that many of the Russian "kulaks" were money-lenders.

Nehru is plain-spoken also with regard to police methods. His own mother, when an old lady, was knocked down in a police charge in 1932, and was hit repeatedly on the head. She was laid at the roadside insensible. Her son was in jail at the time; and when she came to see him a month later, she was still bandaged, though full of joy and pride at having shared in the privilege of suffering for India.

Later, when his dearly loved wife was dying, after eighteen years of married life, incredible harshness and obtuseness was shown by the police authorities in preventing his seeing her. Suggestions were made to him that if he were to give an assurance to keep off politics he might be released from jail to be with his wife. The condition was impossible; but his wife grew more and more ill. When at last he was allowed to see her, though she was almost unable to speak, she whispered, "What is this about your giving an assurance to Government? Don't give it!"

Nehru's conviction that nothing but the total ending of imperialism can meet the needs of India is thus founded not only on a reasoned system of thought, but also on deep feelings that have their root in personal experience of what imperialism does and is from the point of view of the under-dog. He had passed his youth in this country, and had become popular and admired. Then he returned to India, and almost at once stepped into a position of national leadership, owing to his father's great influence as well as to his own qualities. Then he returned to this country, with his wife and child, and was unfortunately the victim of two especially heartless and cruel affronts in London on account of his colour. In this case our race-snobbery "caught a Tartar"; and Nehru went back to India resolved that he would never cease working till he got the imperial painter cut! It will be in place to insist once more that courtesy to guests from abroad, whose complexion happens to differ from our own, is of the first importance to a people assuming any type of international obligations!

Nehru feels himself incalculably indebted to England for what she gave him during his youth. He assures us that, as he looks into his heart, he finds there no bitterness and no anger against the English people. But he dislikes and resents English imperialism, and English capitalism, and the way in which India is exploited by the ruling class of Britain. He comments pointedly on the post-war boom period, when "the average dividend in the jute or cotton mills exceeded a hundred per cent. and was often 150 per cent. per annum." * All these huge profits went to the owners and shareholders, whilst the workers continued to live in wretched hovels and even their women had hardly clothes enough to wear. Therefore for the ending of the poverty of her people Nehru desires the ending of imperialism, and the coming of Socialism.

The two great leaders of modern India, Gandhi and Nehru, are typical of the whole Indian scene: the one with his eyes on the past: the other with his eyes on the future. Both alike are certain that the time has come when at whatever cost—even

* In this same period it is reckoned that for every £100 sent home in dividends, etc., by the jute mills, only £12 was paid in wages to the workers.

at the risk of civil war, or of falling into the maw of Japan—India must become independent. In many ways British rule has been good; but it has not been good enough; it has lead to appalling miseries. The time has come when it must cease, and another way be tried, however steep and hard.

This is the real Indian Crisis. It can only be met as the British people become willing to be true to their own great past, and to trust freedom, at whatever cost.

XXV

SUMMING-UP

To MEET the Crisis in India this book suggests:—

(1) *Mass-education:* especially in the Indian States.
(2) *Constitutions*, in the Indian States.
(3) *Collectivization*, especially in agriculture, also as soon as possible in industry, to solve the problem of poverty, indebtedness, unemployment.
(4) *Democracy*, based not on communal representation (with its inevitable consequence, division and civil warfare), but on large multi-member constituencies, with reservation of seats to ensure the representation of minorities:
(5) *Federalism*, with a very wide measure of devolution to the Provinces: the Federal Legislature to be elected democratically both by the British-Indian Provinces and by the Indian States:
(6) *The Ending of Imperialism:*
(7) As immediate steps, the calling at once of a democratically-elected *Constituent Assembly* (the elected representatives to come both from British India and the Indian States), to make an All-India *Constitution*: and the entrusting of the government of India to a *National Government* set up under that Constitution.

We have before us at present (1943) a situation in which the imperial power has offered India self-government, on a pattern to be chosen by India herself, but after the war. This offer has however been vitiated by the contemplation of the splitting of India into an indefinite number of separate national states, Hindustan, Pakistan, and the areas ruled by various Princes or combinations of Princes, each independent and sovereign, and all bound soon to be at war with one another.

Could confession of failure, after two centuries of imperialism be more abjectly complete, quite apart from all considerations of an ever-deepening poverty and an ever more rapacious capitalism of money-lenders, land-owners and industrial magnates?

INDEX